Building English Vocabulary with Etymology from Latin

Book I

Peter R. Beaven

Building English Vocabulary with Etymology from Latin
Book I
Peter R. Beaven

Editor:
Katharine Webster

Contributors:
Nicia Gruener, Paulette Ghassibi
Stephen E. Stapczynski, Dominic M. Brown
S. James Boumil III, Nikhil Deliwala

Version 5.2 Revised August 29 2018

Published by
The Cheshire Press
an imprint of The Cheshire Group
Andover, MA 01810
www.cheshirepress.com

All rights reserved. No part of this book may be reproduced or transmitted in any form or by any means without the express written consent of the author, except for the inclusion of quotations in reviews.

Copyright © 2005-2008 by Beaven & Associates

ISBN: 978-0-9987465-0-0

Registration Number / Date TX0006858639 / 2007-08-20

Printed in the United States of America

Beaven & Associates
3 Dundee Park, #202 A
Andover, MA 01810
Tel.: 978 475-5487
www.beavenandassociates.com

Beaven, Peter R.
Building English Vocabulary with Etymology from Latin
Book I

Table of Contents

Preface 5

Lesson I: 7
   Ab-, Abs-, A- 7
Lesson II: 15
   Ad-, Ac-, Af-, Ag-, An-, Ap-, As-, ... 15
Lesson III: 24
   Ambi-, Ante- 24
Lesson IV: 29
   Bene-, Bi- 29
Lesson V: 35
   Circum-, Contra- 35
Lesson VI: 41
   Co-, Col-, Com-, Con-, Cor- 41

Test 1 49

Lesson VII: 53
   De- 53
Lesson VIII: 61
   Dis-, Duo- 61
Lesson IX: 69
   Ex-, Equi-, Extra- 69
Lesson X: 77
   In-, Il-, Im-, Ir- 77
Lesson XI: 85
   Il-, Im-, In-, Ir- 85

Test 2 93

Lesson XII: 98
   Inter-, Intra- 98
Lesson XIII: 105
   Magnus-, Mal-, Multi- 105
Lesson XIV: 113
   Ob-, Omni- 113
Lesson XV: 119
   Per- 119
Lesson XVI: 125
   Post, Pre-, Prim- 125

Test 3 133
Lesson XVII: 137
   Pro- 137

Lesson XVIII: 145
   Re-, Retro- 145
Lesson XIX: 151
   Se-, Super- 151
Lesson XX: 157
   Sub- 157
Lesson XXI: 165
   Trans-, Tri-, Ultra-, Uni-, Vice- 165

Test 4 173

Appendix A 177

Quiz 1 178
Quiz 2 179
Quiz 3 180
Quiz 4 181

Answer Key:

Lesson I–V 182
Lesson VI 183

Test 1 183

Lesson VII 183
Lesson VIII–XI 184

Test 2 185

Lesson XII–XIII 185
Lesson XIV–XVI 186

Test 3 187

Lesson XVII–XVIII 187
Lesson XIX–XXI 188

Test 4 188

Quizzes 1-4 189

Index 190

Etymology in Building English Vocabulary

The word "etymology" refers to tracing the origin and historical development of words in a language. How is a given word derived from an earlier word or words in a native or foreign language?

Just as we can "parse" or break up a sentence into parts of speech - noun, verb, adjective, adverb, etc. - so we can deconstruct a given word into its constituent meaning elements and trace their origins. For example, the word "etymology" consists of an original Greek root "etymon" - meaning "an earlier form of the same word" - and the Greek "logos" - meaning "word" or "speech", which took on the later form "-ology" - meaning "study of." So, there we have the etymology of the word "etymology."

Studying the etymology of vocabulary words reveals repeated word-formation patterns, so that we can dissect or guess the meanings of unfamiliar words based on their constituent prefixes and roots that we have encountered earlier. For example, by knowing that the prefix "pre-" means "before" or "ahead" and that "dict" is rooted in "speaking" or "saying," we can surmise that "predict" means to foretell or talk about something before it happens.

The English language is built primarily from the Anglo-Saxon (Germanic), Latin, and Greek languages. Historically, the Angles and Saxons drove out the original Celtic inhabitants and occupied Britain, and after a few brief occupations by the Roman legions, in 1066 the tribes were defeated by the Norman leader William the Conqueror, who spoke French - a language derived almost entirely from Latin. Over time, the Germanic and Latinate languages blended to become what we know as English.

Because Latin is such a fundamental basis of English and because Latin is built from a regular system of "reusable" prefixes and roots, studying these elements makes learning vocabulary more efficient. Instead of learning word meanings in isolation, by learning a standard set of Latin prefixes and common roots we can "mix and match" to learn several new words or variations. The study of etymology thus can accelerate the expansion of our vocabulary while helping us appreciate how meanings and usages have evolved.

For example, knowing that the root "gress" means "step" or "advance", and knowing a series of prefixes, we can deduce word meanings:

Prefix	Meaning	Example
"ad"	= to, toward	address ("g" in "gress" becomes a "d")
"co, con"	= together	congress (movement together)
"di"	= split	digress (move away from)
"e, ex"	= out of, from	egress (way out, exit)
"in"	= in, into	ingress (way in, entrance)
"pro"	= forward, for	progress (move forward)
"re"	= back	regress (move backward)
"trans"	= across, over	transgress (move across)

So many of the words in English that relate to the intellect, words that make us pause to think and study, come from the Greek. The Roman conquest of Greece and admiration for its culture led to the incorporation of many Greek terms into Latin. So we make a point of studying Greek roots and prefixes as well. For example, the Greek root "pathos" means "feeling" or "suffering", from which come such words as:

"a"	= not	apathy (not caring)
"anti"	= against	antipathy (dislike or hostility)
"em, en"	= into, in	empathy (sharing in another's feeling)
"sym"	= together, with	sympathy (feeling sorrow for another)

In addition, there are other English words based on the same root, such as "pathetic", "pathology", "pathos", and so on.

Consider the common prefixes and cross-connections of the words below:

telecommute	micron	automaton	extrasensory	intercede
telegraph	micrograph	autobiography	extravehicular	intercept
telephone	microphone	automobile	extraterrestrial	interrupt
telescope	microscope	autograph	extraordinary	interdict
television	micromanage	autonomy	extralegal	intervene

or the roots "duc" ("lead"), "fer" ("bear, bring"), "port" ("carry") and "vers" ("turn") as below:

aqueduct	confer	report	converse
conduct	defer	deport	diverse
deduce	refer	transport	reverse
duct	transfer	teleport	adverse
ductile	prefer	airport	perverse
educate	offer	purport	obverse
induce		export	averse
produce		import	inverse
seduce		comport	transverse
viaduct		support	controversy

In the series Building English Vocabulary, a student discovers that from just one Latin or Greek root springs an exponential growth in his vocabulary, sharpened tools to articulate the written or spoken word. A broader knowledge of English leads him to greater ties to the shared cognates of French, Spanish, Italian, and Greek. A stronger grasp of English brings a deeper understanding of the plays of Shakespeare, the novels of Dickens, the essays of Emerson, the poetry of Emily Dickinson, or the oratory of Lincoln and Churchill., who as national leaders, marshaled the English language — the former to invoke peace — the latter to evoke resolve for impending battles, the victories of which in the post bellum of the twentieth century helped thrust English into its role as the lingua franca of the modern world.

Lesson I:
Ab-, Abs-, A-

AB-, ABS-
from, away from

abdicate, abduct, abhor, abject, abjure, abominate, abrasion, abrogate, abrupt, abscess, abscond, absolve, absorb, abstain, abstemious, abstruse, abuse, averse, avert, avocation

Word Definitions

abdicate
    v. to renounce the throne; to fail to fulfill or undertake (a duty)
    "Queen Elizabeth may <u>abdicate</u> the throne to her son, Charles."
    abdication (n.)
    abdicare: ab- away + *dicare* to declare

abduct
    v. to take (someone) away illegally by force or deception; kidnap
    "Paris <u>abducted</u> Helen from Sparta to Troy."
    abduction (n.)
    abducere to lead away: *ab-* away + *ducere* to lead

abhor
    v. to regard with loathing or detest
    "Gandhi was said to <u>abhor</u> violence."
    abhorrere: ab- away from + *horrere* to shudder

abject
    adj. miserable; hopeless
    "Starving, disease-ridden refugees in Niger live <u>abject</u> lives."
    abjection (n.), abjectly (adv.)
    abicere: ab- away + *jacere* to throw

abjure
    v. to solemnly renounce (a belief or claim); to give up or abstain from
    "Priests must <u>abjure</u> marriage and remain celibate."
    abjuration (n.)
    abjurare: ab- away + *jurare* to swear

LESSON I: AB-, ABS-, A-

abominate
v. to regard with hatred; to detest
"Indiana Jones <u>abominated</u> Nazis." *abomination (n.)*
abominari to detest; to avoid (as a bad omen): *ab-* away, from + *ominari* to prophesy

abrasion
n. the action of, process of, or result of wearing away by friction and rubbing; a scrape
"A slip on the asphalt caused the man to suffer a knee <u>abrasion</u>."
abradere: *ab-* away + *radere* to scrape, to shave

abrogate
v. to cancel, repeal, or violate (especially a law or agreement)
"The North Koreans' atomic test <u>abrogated</u> the weapons treaty."
abrogation (n.)
abrogare to revoke, repeal, or cancel: *ab-* away + *rogare* to ask, to invite

abrupt
adj. sudden and unexpected; brief to the point of rudeness, curt
"Feeling suddenly ill, the diner <u>abruptly</u> left the table." *abruptly (n.)*
abrumpere to break off, to sever: *ab-* away + *rumpere* to break

abscess
n. a swollen area within body tissue, containing an accumulation of pus
"The untreated blister became an infected <u>abscess</u>."
abscedere to go away; to form an abscess: *abs-* away, from + *cedere* to go

abscond
v. to flee surreptitiously after wrongdoing
"The thief <u>absconded</u> with the bank's money." *abscondere* to hide: *abs-* away + *condere* to put, to bury

absolve
v. to declare (someone) free from guilt or responsibility "The suspect was <u>absolved</u> when his alibi was confirmed."
absolvere to free, to release, to acquit: *ab-* from + *solvere* to loosen

absorb
v. to soak up (liquid or another substance); to assimilate (a lesser entity) into a larger one
"Distracted by a CD player, the pupil did not <u>absorb</u> the lesson."
absorbere to swallow, to suck: *ab-* from + *sorbere* to suck in

abstain
v. to refrain from doing something
"Mormons <u>abstain</u> from drinking alcohol."
abstinere to withhold; to fast: *ab-* from + *tenere* to hold

abstemious
adj. indulging only very moderately in something, especially food and drink
"Monks eat <u>abstemiously</u> to avoid the sin of gluttony."
abstemiously (adv.)
abstemius sober, moderate: *abs-* from + *temetum* strong liquor + *-ous*

abstruse
adj. difficult to understand
"The Kabala is a mystical and <u>abstruse</u> book."
abstrusely (adv.)
abstrudere to conceal: *abs-* from + *trudere* to push

LESSON I: AB-, ABS-, A-

abuse
v. to misuse or use badly
n. improper use or treatment
"Whipping a child as punishment constitutes physical abuse."
abuti to waste, to abuse: *ab-* away + *uti* to use

averse
adj. strongly disliking or opposed
"Averse to getting wet, cats nonetheless are good swimmers."
avertere: *ab-* away + *vertere* to turn

avert
v. to prevent or ward off; to turn away (one's eyes or thoughts)
"By reacting quickly and veering the car, he averted an accident."
avertere: *ab-* away + *vertere* to turn

avocation
n. a hobby or minor occupation
"Model railroading is a popular avocation."
avocational (adj.)
avocare to call away: *ab-* away + *vocare* to call < *vocatio* job, calling

Exercise A

Fill in the blanks in the sentences below with the correct form of a word in the scroll above.

1. During the Civil War, an injured soldier who lacked medical treatment often developed a festering _____ in his wound.

2. In *Risky Business,* when Joel Goodman's parents leave on a weekend trip, they _____ their parental authority by leaving their teenage son home alone.

3. The Al Qaeda terrorists lured the American journalist away from safety in order to _____ him.

4. Despite the millions of dollars designated annually for foreign aid to third world nations, thousands of people in those countries live in _____ poverty.

5. When Suzanne received the sacrament of Confirmation, she said she would _____ the false promises of Satan.

6. Many Democrats _____ the practice of capital punishment.

LESSON I: AB-, ABS-, A-

7. Judy _____ from eating an ice cream sundae before dinner, because she did not want to spoil her appetite.

8. Sue instilled her own _____ habits in her children by eating like a bird in front of them.

9. Division proved _____ to Ms. Smith's fourth grade class because they had failed to master multiplication.

10. Kate _____ the privilege of swimming in the public pool by not showering first and failing to wear a bathing cap.

11. Sheila was not _____ to dancing with Bill. In fact, she rather wished he would ask her to dance.

12. When Martha caught Carlos staring at her, Carlos quickly _____ his eyes and blushed.

13. A retired soccer star, Raul now works as an accountant, but his _____ is coaching soccer.

14. I never make treaties when playing the board game *Risk*, because my opponent will _____ them and attack me when I least expect it.

15. Upon seeing a squirrel in the middle of the road, the driver made an _____ evasive maneuver to avoid hitting it.

16. Upon spying the freshly baked chocolate chip cookies, Timmy filled his pockets with them and _____ with the booty to the safety of his closet.

17. When Joe confessed that he had lied to his mother, the priest _____ Joe of his sin.

18. When Karen spilled cranberry juice on the kitchen counter, she used a wad of paper towels to _____ the liquid.

19. Although Emmanuel's favorite movie is *The Shining*, his wife and daughter have never seen it. They _____ horror movies.

20. The cement levee protecting the ocean-front cottage was crumbling after years of _____ by high tides and pounding waves.

LESSON I: AB-, ABS-, A-

Exercise B

Match the word with the letter of its definition.

1. abdicate
2. abduct
3. abhor
4. abject
5. abjure
6. abominate
7. abrasion
8. abrogate
9. abrupt
10. abscess
11. abscond
12. absolve
13. absorb
14. abstain
15. abstemious
16. abstruse
17. abuse
18. averse
19. avert
20. avocation

a) prevent from happening
b) challenging to comprehend
c) declare innocent of guilt or sin
d) hobby or minor occupation
e) carry off (a person) unlawfully
f) leave hurriedly to avoid arrest
g) result of an infection
h) soak up
i) opposed to
j) result of wearing away
k) shrink away from with disgust
l) misuse
m) sparing in the consumption of food
n) relinquish authority
o) swear to reject
p) cancel a law or treaty
q) feel intense hatred toward
r) sudden (change in action or manner)
s) miserable, hopeless
t) refrain from doing

Exercise C

Circle the letter of the definition that best fits the meaning of the word.

1. **abdicate**
   a. shrink away from with disgust
   b. relinquish authority
   c. steal away with
   d. support faithfully
   e. divert blame

2. **abduct**
   a. carry off unlawfully
   b. pardon of guilt
   c. disagree with
   d. eat voraciously
   e. plagiarize

3. **abhor**
   a. eat with great enthusiasm
   b. draw in the essence of
   c. shrink away from with disgust
   d. spit out quickly
   e. tease mercilessly

4. **abject**
   a. miserable, hopeless
   b. standing out from surroundings
   c. unable to be deterred
   d. unusual, offbeat
   e. quick to anger

LESSON I: AB-, ABS-, A-

5. **abjure**
   a. to judge
   b. swear to reject
   c. deliberate and decide upon
   d. lose grip on an object
   e. obscure the truth

6. **abominate**
   a. scold
   b. detest
   c. destroy
   d. cancel
   e. terminate

7. **abrasion**
   a. reaction of waves
   b. result of wearing away
   c. taste for sweetness
   d. feelings of others
   e. action of pushing against an external force

8. **abrogate**
   a. violate law or treaty
   b. run away
   c. combine into one
   d. begin negotiations
   e. spoil or rot

9. **abrupt**
   a. occurring during something else
   b. sudden (change in action or manner)
   c. intruding upon rudely
   d. splintered or shattered
   e. variegated

10. **abscess**
    a. determination of value
    b. amount beyond what is necessary
    c. result of an infection
    d. entrance of a building
    e. growth within the intestinal tract

11. **abscond**
    a. steal away
    b. eat in secrecy
    c. scold secretly
    d. cover up
    e. eliminate from consideration

12. **absolve**
    a. disintegrate
    b. soak up the essence of
    c. declare innocent of guilt or sin
    d. be unable to solve
    e. reason logically

13. **absorb**
    a. soak up
    b. block out
    c. eliminate
    d. recognize
    e. withstand

14. **abstain**
    a. shrink away from with disgust
    b. get a hold of
    c. refrain from doing
    d. spill
    e. stay away from

15. **abstemious**
    a. very hot and humid
    b. sparing in the consumption of food and drink
    c. miserly and cheap
    d. perceptive to details
    e. sensitive to injustice

16. **abstruse**
    a. protruding
    b. challenging to comprehend
    c. lacking quickness of perception or intellect
    d. hidden from view
    e. simplistic or crude in nature

LESSON I: AB-, ABS-, A-

17. **abuse**
    a. misuse
    b. employ
    c. pay attention
    d. ignore
    e. avoid

18. **averse**
    a. verbose, wordy
    b. pertaining to
    c. opposed to
    d. stingy or miserly
    e. circular or cyclical

19. **avert**
    a. display openly
    b. prevent from happening
    c. turn toward
    d. distract someone's attention
    e. delay from occurring

20. **avocation**
    a. hobby or minor occupation
    b. abraded surface
    c. song or work of art
    d. figure of speech
    e. formal letter

Exercise D

Solve the crossword puzzle:

Across
1. Sudden and unexpected; brief to the point of rudeness; curt. 2. To refrain from doing something. 3. To prevent or ward off; to turn away (one's eyes or thoughts). 4. To regard with loathing or detest. 5. A swollen area within body tissue, containing an accumulation of pus. 7. Miserable, hopeless; (of something bad) complete and utter. 8. To renounce the throne; to fail to fulfill or undertake (a duty). 9. Indulging only very moderately in something, especially food and drink. 11. To declare (someone) free from guilt or responsibility. 12. To misuse or use badly. 13. To cancel, repeal, or violate (especially a law or agreement).

Down
1. To soak up (liquid or another substance); to assimilate (a lesser entity) into a larger one. 3. To leave hurriedly and secretly after wrongdoing. 4. To solemnly renounce (a belief or claim); to give up or abstain from. 6. To take (someone) away illegally by force or deception; kidnap. 7. The action of, process of, or result of wearing away by friction and rubbing; a scrape. 8. Difficult to understand. 9. To regard with hatred. 10. A hobby or minor occupation. 11. Strongly disliking or opposed.

Lesson II:
Ad-, Ac-, Af-, Ag-, An-, Ap-, As-, At-

**AC-, AD-, AF-, AG-,
AN-, AP-, AS-, AT-
to, forward, toward**

accord, adaptable, adequate, adhere, ad hoc, adjacent, adjoin, admonish, adopt, advent, adversary, adverse, affliction, aggregation, annexation, appear, appease, arraignment, assimilate, assumption

Word Definitions

accord
v. to give or grant someone (power or recognition)
n. an official agreement or treaty; a meeting of the minds
"Hostilities ceased when the two sides reached a peace <u>accord</u>."
ad- to + *cor-, cord* heart, mind, spirit

adaptable
adj. able to adjust to new conditions
"Humans are <u>adaptable</u> to all manner of climates."
adaptability (n.)
adaptably (ad.)
adaptare to adjust, to modify: *ad-* to + *aptare* to fit < *aptus* fitting

adequate
adj. satisfactory or acceptable; sufficient
"His success proved he was <u>adequate</u> to the task."
adequacy (n.)
adequately (adv.)
adaequare to make equal, to level: *ad-* to + *aequus* equal

adhere	v. to stick fast to; to believe in and follow the practices of; to represent truthfully and in detail "Orthodox Jews adhere to strict dietary laws." *adhaerere* to adhere, to cling: *ad-* to + *haerere* to stick
ad hoc	adj. & adv. formed, arranged, or done for one particular purpose only "The ad hoc Prom Committee dissolved after the dance." *ad-* to + *hoc* this
adjacent	adj. next to or adjoining something else; having a common vertex or a common side. "Massachusetts is adjacent to five other states." *adjacency (n.)* *adjacere* to lie near: *ad-* to + *jacere* to lie down, to sleep
adjoin	v. to be next to and joined with "The House of Representatives adjoins the Senate building." *adjungere* to join to, to support: *ad-* to + *jungere* to join
admonish	v. to warn; to reprove firmly; to advise or urge earnestly "The cop admonished the speeder to slow down." *admonition (n.), admonishment (n.)* *admonere* to warn: *ad-* (expressing intensity) + *monere* to advise, to remind
adopt	v. to legally take (another's child) and bring up as one's own; to choose; to assume (an attitude or position) *adoptable (adj.)* "The accused adopted a defensive attitude." *adoptare* to adopt, to select: *ad-* to + *optare* to choose
advent	n. the arrival of a notable person, event or development "Leaves turning color signal the advent of fall." *advenire* to arrive, to be brought: *ad-* to + *venire* to come
adversary	n. an opponent "George Bush overcame his adversary, John Kerry, and was reelected." *adversarial (adj)* *advertere* to turn toward, to face: *ad-* to + *vertere* to turn
adverse	adj. preventing success or development; unfavorable or harmful "Despite his adverse circumstances, the impoverished boy went to college." *adversely (adv.)* *advertere* to turn toward, to face: *ad-* to + *vertere* to turn
affliction	n. a cause or condition of pain or harm; an illness "For the elderly, flu can be a deadly affliction." *affligere* to knock down, to weaken: *ad-* down + *fligere* to strike

LESSON II:AD-, AC-, AF-, AG-, AN-, AP-, AS-, AT-

aggregation n. a collection of gathered objects; a whole formed by combining several elements
"The coalition is an aggregation of peace, civil rights and anti-war groups." *aggregare* to herd together: *ad-* towards + *gregare* to collect < *grex, greg-* a flock

annexation n. the action of adding something to a whole; joining onto something
"The annexation of Austria was one of Hitler's first moves."
annex (v.)
annectere to connect: *ad-* to + *nectere* to bind

appear v. to come into sight; to arrive; to seem or look
"Blackberries appear red when they are unripe."
apparere to appear; to occur: *ad-* toward + *parere* to come into view

appease v. to placate (someone) by acceding to their demands
"He appeased his father by studying engineering as well as art."
appeasement (n.)
ad- to + *pax* peace

arraignment n. a court hearing to bring formal charges against someone
"At his arraignment, the man was charged and pleaded not guilty."
arraign (v.)
adrationare to call to account: *ad-* to + *ratio, ration-* reason, account

assimilate v. to take in and fully understand; to absorb and digest
"Some Jews fear assimilation with gentiles may weaken Judaism."
assimilation (n.)
assimilare to absorb, to make similar to: *ad-* to + *similis* like

assumption n. a belief or fact that is taken for granted; the act of taking responsibility or control
"The U.S.'s assumption of third world debts is controversial."
assume (v.)
ad- (expressing intensity) + *sumere* to accept, to take up

EXERCISE A

Fill in the blanks in the sentences below with the correct form of a word in the scroll above.

1. Some childless couples wish to _____ a baby, while others prefer an older child.

2. The accused was arrested when he attempted to flee the country before the date of his _____.

17

LESSON II: AD-, AC-, AF-, AG-, AN-, AP-, AS-, AT-

3. Few people noticed Jeff's presence in class. When he spoke, he seemed to _____ out of thin air.

4. Many people make the _____ that Dr. Reddenbacher is a man, but upon meeting her, they realize she is not.

5. Nancy and Jeffrey agreed to disagree, and reached an _____ to refrain from arguing for the rest of the day.

6. Sarossa's parents _____ her against spending her weekend with friends at the beach instead of with her books at the library.

7. Since the rain jacket had a removable fleece lining for insulation, it was _____ for use in any climate or season.

8. David wished he had a larger apartment, but his current one was _____

9. Never underestimate the ability of America to _____ a new group of immigrants that lands on its shores.

10. Tuberculosis, once a deadly _____, is now only a threat to the elderly or impoverished.

11. Each year the generous handyman carried out various _____ projects for the sickly old woman next door.

12. *Spiderman*, starring Toby McGuire as the web-slinger and Willem Dafoe as his _____, the Green Goblin, spawned a blockbuster sequel.

13. Jerry McGuire was jolly because he had done all his Christmas shopping before the _____ of the holiday season.

14. The menagerie on Gwyneth's window sill was an _____ of animal figurines from all over the world.

15. In order to _____ the voters, the politician compromised his principles.

16. The United States' _____ of Texas resulted from a bloody war with Mexico.

LESSON II: AD-, AC-, AF-, AG-, AN-, AP-, AS-, AT-

17. Though tempted to keep the paper bag full of money, Sarah _____ to her principles and tracked down the rightful owner.

18. Because the room where the baby was screaming _____ Mr. and Mrs. Bennifer's, the baby's wails woke them.

19. While Mrs. Kennedy encouraged her students to comment on each other's papers, _____ criticism was unacceptable.

20. The SUV was too large for the parking space at Tan-O-Rama, so it ended up occupying half of an _____ space.

LESSON II: AD-, AC-, AF-, AG-, AN-, AP-, AS-, AT-

EXERCISE B

Match the word with the letter of its definition.

1. accord
2. adaptable
3. adequate
4. adhere
5. ad hoc
6. adjacent
7. adjoin
8. admonish
9. adopt
10. advent
11. adversary
12. adverse
13. affliction
14. aggregation
15. annexation
16. appear
17. appease
18. arraignment
19. assimilate
20. assumption

a) an enemy
b) adding something to a whole
c) to scold
d) an agreement
e) to come into view
f) hostile
g) the arrival of a date
h) to satisfy or placate
i) to absorb into a larger whole
j) for a specific purpose
k) to connect or to be situated next to
l) to stick closely to (something)
m) bordering
n) court hearing to bring charges
o) flexible
p) sufficient
q) something taken to be true
r) an ailment causing physical or mental suffering
s) to choose for oneself
t) a collection of gathered objects

EXERCISE C

Circle the letter of the definition that best fits the meaning of the bold-faced word.

1. **accord**
   a. difference between similar objects
   b. agreement
   c. respect for someone
   d. heart-shaped flower
   e. wire or string

2. **adaptable**
   a. flexible, able to change
   b. skillful
   c. able to remain ripe for long period of time
   d. willing to work diligently
   e. difficult to detect

LESSON II: AD-, AC-, AF-, AG-, AN-, AP-, AS-, AT-

3. **adequate**
   a. superior
   b. sufficient
   c. ancient
   d. confusing
   e. unnecessary

4. **adhere**
   a. tell truthfully
   b. consider carefully
   c. attach to
   d. withstand
   e. work together

5. **ad hoc**
   a. for a specific purpose
   b. unplanned and whimsical
   c. careless
   d. incomprehensible
   e. serious

6. **adjacent**
   a. distant
   b. bordering
   c. joking
   d. similar
   e. rude

7. **adjoin**
   a. disperse amongst a group
   b. add to a total or whole
   c. connect to or to be next to
   d. accept into a group
   e. reject tentatively

8. **admonish**
   a. lie under oath
   b. deviate from an accepted norm
   c. allow
   d. deter
   e. scold

9. **adopt**
   a. give control of
   b. move forward
   c. control
   d. please
   e. choose for oneself

10. **advent**
    a. arrival of a date
    b. position of superiority
    c. new beginning
    d. the time at which a law takes effect
    e. new idea or invention

11. **adversary**
    a. person of similar circumstances
    b. comrade
    c. enemy or foe
    d. deceased relative
    e. merchant of weapons

12. **adverse**
    a. hostile
    b. fearful
    c. durable
    d. despicable
    e. admirable

13. **affliction**
    a. mirror image of an object
    b. repentance of a minor sin
    c. ailment causing physical or mental suffering
    d. change in tone or manner or speech
    e. unpopular monarch

14. **aggregation**
    a. gathering of objects into a collection
    b. group of people that share similar beliefs
    c. herd of cattle on a dairy farm
    d. intense anger with a situation
    e. sorting a group into like parts

15. **annexation**
    a. state of relaxation
    b. act of adding something to a whole
    c. added on piece of a whole
    d. member of a splintered group
    e. destruction of land

LESSON II: AD-, AC-, AF-, AG-, AN-, AP-, AS-, AT-

16. **appear**
    a. consider carefully
    b. restore
    c. come into view
    d. receive punishment
    e. deceive

17. **appease**
    a. confront
    b. remove from power
    c. please all people
    d. surrender
    e. satisfy, to make calm

18. **arraignment**
    a. rapid decision
    b. court hearing to bring charges
    c. act of being arrested
    d. holding cell for an accused during trial
    e. previously decided upon set of conditions

19. **assimilate**
    a. disappear from view
    b. connect two unrelated machines
    c. disguise
    d. get together with friends for a cause
    e. absorb into a larger whole

20. **assumption**
    a. fa<ade, front
    b. idea once popular, but now disproved
    c. something one takes to be true
    d. major decision
    e. necessary sacrifice for a greater good

LESSON II: AD-, AC-, AF-, AG-, AN-, AP-, AS-, AT-

Exercise D

Solve the crossword puzzle:

Across

3. To come into sight; to arrive; to seem. 5. Preventing success or development; unfavorable. 8. To stick fast to; to believe in and follow the practices of. 9. The arrival of a notable person or event. 10. Able to adjust to new conditions. 12. An opponent. 13. Something taken for granted; the action of taking responsibility or control. 14. To warn; to reprove gently, but earnestly. 15. Satisfactory or acceptable.

Down

1. To give or grant someone (power or recognition); an agreement. 2. To legally take (another's child) and bring up as one's own; to choose for oneself; to assume (an attitude or position). 3. A court hearing to bring formal charges. 4. Next to something else. 7. To placate (someone) by acceding to their demands. 8. The act of adding something to a whole; joining onto something. 10. A collection of gathered objects. 11. To take in and fully understand; to absorb and digest. 13. A cause or condition of pain or harm; an illness. 14. To be next to and joined with.

Lesson III:
Ambi-, Ante-

AMBI-
both

ANTE-
before

ambidextrous, ambiguous, ambivalent, antebellum, antecedent, antedate, antediluvian, ante meridian, anterior, anticipate

Word Definitions

ambidextrous **adj.** able to use the right and left hands equally well
"Grover Cleveland, who was <u>ambidextrous</u>, could write with two hands simultaneously."
ambidexterity (n.)
ambi- both + *dexter* right-handed

ambiguous **adj.** having more than one meaning, open to different interpretations
"The word 'sanction' is <u>ambiguous</u> as it has two opposite meanings."
ambiguus doubtful, changeable < *ambigere* to hesitate, to doubt: *ambi-* both + *agere* to drive, to act

ambivalent **adj.** having mixed feelings or opinions about something or someone
"The college student was <u>ambivalent</u> about marriage."
ambivalence (n.)
ambi- both + *valere* to be strong, to prevail < *valentia* vigor, strength

antebellum **adj.** occurring or existing before a war (especially the U.S. Civil War)
"Slavery was pervasive in the <u>antebellum</u> South."
ante- before + *bellum* war

antecedent	**n.** a thing that existed before or logically precedes another; the noun to which a pronoun refers **adj.** preceding in time or order "The Boston Massacre was an antecedent to the Boston Tea Party." *antecedere* to precede; to surpass or excel: *ante-* before + *cedere* to go
antedate	**v.** to come before in date; to precede "The War of 1812 antedates the Civil War." *ante-* before + *dare* to give
antediluvian	**adj.** of or belonging to the time before the biblical Flood; antiquated "My grandmother has antediluvian ideas about etiquette and dating." *ante-* before + *diluvium* deluge < *diluere* to wash away
ante meridian	**adj.** of or relating to or taking place in the morning; A.M. "Breakfast is normally an antemeridian meal." *ante-* before + *meridies* noon
anterior	**adj.** frontal or near the front (the opposite of posterior); earlier in time "An anterior human view shows the face and chest." (comparative of *ante-* before)
anticipate	**v.** to be aware of and prepare for; to look forward to "Hannibal was able to anticipate the Roman moves and thwart them." *anticipare* to take before: *ante-* before + *capere* to take hold, to grasp

EXERCISE A

Fill in the blanks in the sentences below with the correct form of a word in the scroll above.

1. People learning English as a second language struggle with _____ words such as "fair" and "tire."

2. The ant's thorax is _____ to its abdomen.

3. Cartographers around the world are debating the authenticity of a world map circa 1450, because the map includes an area marked, "New World," yet purports to _____ Christopher Columbus' first transatlantic voyage.

4. Frederick Douglass, the former slave who became one of America's most respected poets and speakers, was born in the _____ South.

5. Sarah was _____ about whether to go abroad for the summer or help her grandfather on his struggling dairy farm.

6. On Han's walking tour of the Mayan ruins, the guide pointed out _____ tools treasured by the ancient culture.

LESSON III: AMB!-, ANTE-

7. Some _____ artists write with one hand and draw with the other.

8. Seeing the puzzled look on Jessica's face, Nick explained that _____ was a term that meant "before noon".

9. Many textbooks prefer to use the pronoun "one" rather than "he" or "she" because the gender of the _____ noun is undetermined.

10. Marquez didn't _____ the holiday bonus he received from his boss, because he had begun working for Dynacorp just a few weeks earlier.

EXERCISE B

Match the word with the letter of its definition.

1. ambidextrous
2. ambiguous
3. ambivalent
4. antebellum
5. antecedent
6. antedate
7. antediluvian
8. ante meridian
9. anterior
10. anticipate

a) thing that logically precedes another
b) before noon
c) antiquated
d) having more than one meaning or interpretation
e) frontal
f) expect
g) having mixed feelings
h) prior to war
i) able to use both left and right hands equally
j) precede in time

EXERCISE C

Circle the letter of the definition which best fits the meaning of the word.

1. **ambidextrous**
   a. colorblind
   b. facile with both left and right hands
   c. impatient
   d. fond of sport
   e. mountainous

2. **ambiguous**
   a. relating to grandiose things
   b. being abundant and plentiful
   c. having more than one possible meaning or interpretation
   d. coming to fruition
   e. pertaining to sea life

LESSON III: AMB!-, ANTE-

3. **ambivalent**
   a. very strong emotions
   b. having mixed feelings
   c. perverted
   d. two-sided
   e. introverted

4. **antebellum**
   a. prior to war
   b. ugly
   c. protesting war
   d. rebellious
   e. describing plantation life

5. **antecedent**
   a. dramatic exit
   b. thing that logically precedes another
   c. unprecedented
   d. medical term for a "baby tooth"
   e. progression in thought or action

6. **antedate**
   a. stand someone up
   b. term for February 29th
   c. precede in time
   d. cancel
   e. contradict someone

7. **antediluvian**
   a. end point of the large intestine
   b. futuristic
   c. neurotic
   d. opposing the Diluvian school of thought
   e. antiquated

8. **ante meridian**
   a. bottommost ten feet of the ocean
   b. highest point or stage of development
   c. near the poles
   d. before noon
   e. point between high and low tides

9. **anterior**
   a. nearer the front
   b. inside
   c. back end of an animal
   d. last segment of an ant's body
   e. small bone inside your ear

10. **anticipate**
    a. eat with fervor
    b. greet with excitement
    c. expect
    d. steal
    e. review

Exercise D

Solve the crossword puzzle:

Across
4. Nearer the front (the opposite of posterior); occurring earlier. 5. Of or belonging to the time before the biblical flood; antiquated. 6. Occurring or existing before a particular war (especially the U.S. Civil War). 7. To come before in date; to precede in time.

Down
1. Able to use the right and left hands equally well. 2. To be aware of and prepare for; to look forward to. 4. Having mixed feelings or opinions about something or someone. 6. A thing that existed before or logically precedes another; the noun to which a pronoun refers. 8. Having more than one meaning; open to different interpretations.

Lesson IV:
Bene-, Bi-

BENE-
good, well

BI-
two

benediction, benefactor, beneficent, benevolence, benign, bicameral, biceps, bicuspid, bifurcate, bilateral, bilingual, bipartisan, bisect, bona fide, bonus

benediction	**n.** the utterance or bestowing of a blessing "The Sunday service closed with the minister's benediction." *benedicere* to bless: *bene* well + *dicere* to say
benefactor	**n.** a person who gives money or other help to a person or cause "The secret benefactor gave money to charity anonymously." *bene* good + *facere* to make, to do
beneficent	**adj.** doing good or resulting in good "Bill Gates has been beneficent in giving millions to combat AIDS." *bene* good + *facere* to make, to do
benevolence	**n.** an inclination to perform kind, charitable acts; a kindly act "The Boy Scout showed benevolence in helping the crippled lady." benevolent (adj.) *bene* well + *velle* to wish
benign	**adj.** genial and kindly; of no health risk (opposite of malignant) "A biopsy can determine whether a mole is benign or cancerous." *bene* well + *genus* birth, family, variety
bicameral	**adj.** (of a legislative body) having two legislative houses "A legislature with two houses is called 'bicameral'." *bicameralism (n.)* *bi-* two + *camera* room, chamber
biceps	**n.** the large muscle in the upper arm (which has two points of attachment) "Schwarzenegger's biceps protrude from his short sleeves." *bi-* two + *caput* head

LESSON IV: BENE-, BI-

bicuspid
    adj. having two cusps or points
    n. a tooth with two cusps, especially a human premolar tooth
    "A crescent moon has a bicuspid form."
    bi- two + *cuspis, cuspidis* sharp point

bifurcate
    v. to divide into two branches or forks
    adj. divided into two branches or forks
    "The Ohio River bifurcates into the Allegheny and Monongahela rivers."
    bi- two + *furca* fork

bilateral
    adj. having or relating to two sides
    "The human body evinces bilateral symmetry."
    bi- two + *latus* side

bilingual
    adj. speaking two languages fluently
    "Most Swiss are at least bilingual, speaking German and French."
    bi- two + *lingua* tongue, language

bipartisan
    adj. of or involving the agreement or cooperation of two political parties
    "A constitutional amendment must have bipartisan appeal to pass."
    bipartisanship (n.)
    bi- two + *pars-, part-* part

bisect
    v. to divide into two parts, usually equal
    "The Mississippi River roughly bisects the United States."
    bisector (n.)
    bi- two + *secare* to cut

bona fide
    adj. genuine, real, sincere
    adv. without intention to deceive
    "Was the offer bona fide or merely a hoax?"
    bona good + *fide* faith

bonus
    n. anything given or paid in addition to the expected
    "Cracker Jack traditionally contains a toy as a bonus."
    bonus good

EXERCISE A

Fill in the blanks in the sentences with the proper form of one of the words in the word box.

1. Arnold joined a gym and lifted weights in hopes of making his _____ bigger.

2. Mother Theresa exhibited admirable _____ in her work with the downtrodden and impoverished.

LESSON IV: BENE-, BI-

3. The United States boasts a _____ legislature; Congress is made up of two chambers: the Senate and the House of Representatives.

4. After losing all her baby teeth, Julia noticed that a _____ began to grow next to her molars.

5. At the end of the interfaith service, the minister asked the congregation to bow their heads while he gave the _____.

6. The Montezuma River _____(s) into two smaller tributaries.

7. All the associates at the law firm competed for the holiday _____, given to a single exceptional employee for his or her diligence and effort.

8. After she made her weekly visits to the local nursing home, Hillary felt truly _____.

9. When Miss Winona Ryder was stopped by the plain-clothes detective, she wasn't sure whether or not the man was a _____ police officer.

10. The bill passed unanimously into law because it had _____ support.

11. The dotted yellow line _____ the highway.

12. An isosceles triangle exhibits _____ symmetry.

13. Upon hearing that her tumor was _____, the patient felt tremendous relief.

14. The Museum of Fine Arts in Boston, Massachusetts, recognizes its most generous _____ on a prominent plaque in the lobby.

15. Mr. Banderas grew up in a Spanish-speaking house, but went to an English-speaking school and became _____.

LESSON IV: BENE-, BI-

EXERCISE B

Match the word with the letter of its definition.

1. benediction
2. benefactor
3. beneficent
4. benevolence
5. benign
6. bicameral
7. biceps
8. bicuspid
9. bifurcate
10. bilateral
11. bilingual
12. bipartisan
13. bisect
14. bona fide
15. bonus

a) having two legislative houses
b) person who offers financial support
c) large upper arm muscle
d) in good faith
e) supported by two political parties
f) blessing
g) performing or resulting in good
h) double-pointed tooth
i) posing no threat or danger
j) having two sides
k) having the ability to speak two languages
l) divide into two equal parts
m) good will
n) reward, extra pay
o) split into two; fork

EXERCISE C

Circle the letter of the definition which best fits the meaning of the bold-faced word.

1. **benediction**
   a. omen of good things to come
   b. unusually good luck or fortune
   c. formal speech
   d. blessing
   e. oath a government official must take before taking office

2. **benefactor**
   a. person legally responsible for child
   b. owner of a museum
   c. person released from imprisonment
   d. person who offers financial support
   e. one who is all-knowing

3. **beneficent**
   a. performing acts of kindness
   b. active
   c. hateful
   d. having good luck
   e. estranged

4. **benevolence**
   a. good will
   b. total power
   c. good luck
   d. ill will
   e. peace

LESSON IV: BENE-, BI-

5. **benign**
   a. springing into action
   b. coming into money
   c. knowing danger
   d. posing no threat or danger
   e. threatening

6. **bicameral**
   a. having two lenses
   b. having similar interests
   c. having two legs
   d. having two ethnic heritages
   e. having two distinct legislative houses

7. **biceps**
   a. small muscle in the leg
   b. large upper arm muscle
   c. molar tooth
   d. large muscle in the back
   e. second joint on one's finger

8. **bicuspid**
   a. double pointed tooth
   b. incisor tooth
   c. point at which the surf touches the sand
   d. muscle surrounding one's knee cap
   e. point on the horizon where the sky appears to meet the ocean

9. **bifurcate**
   a. split into three
   b. break into random pieces
   c. separate
   d. divide into parts
   e. split into two; fork

10. **bilateral**
    a. having two sides
    b. having congruent sides
    c. having four sides
    d. having parallel sides
    e. having one side

11. **bilingual**
    a. having the ability to play two instruments
    b. having the ability to read three languages
    c. having the ability to listen to two conversations simultaneously
    d. having the ability to speak two languages
    e. having the ability to translate

12. **bipartisan**
    a. having three opposing sides
    b. having two parties in unequal size
    c. having many parts
    d. possessing the support of two different political parties
    e. having two sharp edges

13. **bisect**
    a. divide an object into two equally sized parts
    b. cut violently
    c. put two pieces together
    d. slice into three equal pieces
    e. divide into two unequal pieces

14. **bona fide**
    a. enlarged
    b. in bad faith
    c. sealed
    d. shrunken
    e. in good faith

15. **bonus**
    a. good deed
    b. reward or prize
    c. short sword
    d. undeserved addition
    e. sworn secret

Exercise D

Solve the crossword puzzle:

Across
1. Having or relating to two sides. 7. The utterance or bestowing of a blessing. 8. Genial and kindly; of no health risk. 9. Anything given or paid in addition to the expected. 10. Involving the agreement or cooperation of two political parties. 11. To divide into two branches or forks. 12. A person who gives money or other help to a person or cause.

Down
1. Having two cusps or points. 2. Speaking two languages fluently. 3. The large muscle in the upper arm. 4. Genuine, real, sincere. 5. (Of a legislative body) having two chambers. 6. Doing good or resulting in good. 7. An inclination to perform kind, charitable acts; a kindly act. 8. To divide into two parts, usually equal.

Lesson V:
Circum-, Contra-

CIRCUM-
around

CONTRA-
against, contrary

circuitous, circulate, circumference, circumlocution, circumnavigate, circumscribe, circumspect, circumstantial, circumvent, contraband, contraceptive, contradict, contrast, contravene, controversy

Word Definitions

circuitous adj. longer than the most direct way, indirect
"State roads follow more circuitous routes than interstates."
circumire to go around: *circum-* around + *ire* to go

circulate v. to move or cause to move around continuously or freely "Harvey discovered that blood circulates through the body." *circulare* to move in a circular path < *circulus* circle

circumference n. the enclosing boundary of a circle; the outer boundary of (something)
"The hermit lives a life of limited circumference."
circumferre to carry around: *circum-* around + *ferre* to carry

circumlocution n. the use of many words where fewer would do; evasive or indirect speech
"'Desist from excessive noise' is a circumlocution for 'Be quiet!'"
circumlocutory (adj.)
circum- around + *loqui* to speak

circumnavigate v. to sail all the way around
"The ship was unable to circumnavigate Australia in a month."
circumnavigation (n.)
circum- around + *navigare* to sail

LESSON V: CIRCUM-, CONTRA-

circumscribe **v.** to restrict, limit; to draw a circle around
"A bed-ridden hospital patient's mobility is <u>circumscribed</u>."
circumscription (n.)
circumscribere to confine; to draw around: *circum-* around + *scribere* to write

circumspect **adj.** cautious or prudent
"The scout was <u>circumspect</u> to avoid traps and Indian attacks."
circumspection (n.)
circum- around + *specere* to look at, to see

circumstantial **adj.** incidental; dependent on circumstances; suggestive, but not definitive
"Fingerprints and a smoking gun linked him to the crime; all the evidence was <u>circumstantial</u>."
circumstare to gather around, to surround: *circum-* around + *stare* to stand

circumvent **v.** to find a way around (an obstacle or problem); to surround
"The politician <u>circumvented</u> the question by asking his own."
circumvention (n.)
circumvenire to encircle; to circumvent: *circum-* around + *venire* to come

contraband **n.** goods that have been imported or exported illegally
adj. prohibited from being imported or exported
"The Border Patrol's task was to seize <u>contraband</u> such as cocaine."
contra- against + *bannus* proclamation, edict, ban

contraceptive **adj.** serving to prevent pregnancy
n. a contraceptive device
"Linen wrappings and sheepskin were early male contraceptives."
contra- against + *concipere* to conceive

contradict **v.** to deny the truth of (a statement) by asserting the opposite
"The laboratory findings <u>contradict</u> the original diagnosis."
contradicere to contradict: *contra-* against + *dicere* to say, to speak

contrast **v.** to differ strikingly
n. the state of being strikingly different from something else
"Parents' and children's attitudes toward curfews usually <u>contrast</u>."
contra- against + *stare* to stand

contravene **v.** to offend against the requirements (of a law, treaty, etc.); to oppose in argument
"Torture of prisoners of war <u>contravenes</u> the Geneva Conventions."
contravenire to oppose: *contra-* against + *venire* to come

controversy **n.** prolonged disagreement or heated debate
"Talk shows with more <u>controversy</u> draw more viewers."
controversial (n.)
contraversus disputed, turned against: *contra-* against + *vertere* to turn

LESSON V: CIRCUM-, CONTRA-

EXERCISE A

Fill in the blanks in the sentences below with the correct form of a word in the scroll above.

1. Students use the formula 2πr to determine the _____ of a circle.

2. It caused quite a _____ when the anti-abortionists demanded equal speaking time at the rally.

3. English students are admonished to stop being verbose if their writing employs _____ rather than clear and concise statements.

4. The beach road was quite _____, meandering around the sand dunes.

5. The general _____ the antiwar speakers by arguing their understanding of international affairs was too superficial to comprehend the necessity of war.

6. In 1522, Magellan's crew became the first to successfully _____ the globe.

7. The criminals were able to _____ government detection of their check schemes for years.

8. Mike kept searching for the right color to _____ with the dark background of the painting.

9. Julia Roberts was _____ about walking to her car in dark parking lots.

10. Miss Estacio taught her health class about _____ so they would know how to prevent pregnancy.

11. To help prevent _____ drugs from entering our borders, we need to increase surveillance and security.

12. From all accounts, the accident was preventable, because the lifeguard had clearly _____ the safe swimming area with a rope.

13. The little girl had the unfortunate habit of _____ her parents' every instruction.

14. During the party, Sam and Paul _____ to meet as many new pledges as possible.

15. Mrs. Roberts decided the crumbs on her son's T-shirt provided sufficient _____ evidence to accuse him of cookie theft.

EXERCISE B

Match the word with the letter of its definition.

1. **circuitous**
2. **circulate**
3. **circumference**
4. **circumlocution**
5. **circumnavigate**
6. **circumscribe**
7. **circumspect**
8. **circumstantial**
9. **circumvent**
10. **contraband**
11. **contraceptive**
12. **contradict**
13. **contrast**
14. **contravene**
15. **controversy**

a) avoid
b) boundary of a circle
c) say the opposite or deny
d) cautious or prudent
e) difference most striking when used in comparison
f) disagreement
g) restrict or limit
h) use of many words when fewer would do
i) illegally smuggled or imported goods
j) oppose
k) indirect, winding
l) sail all the way around
m) pointing indirectly toward a conclusion
n) move continuously or freely
o) method of preventing pregnancy

EXERCISE C

Circle the letter of the definition that best fits the meaning of the bold-faced word.

1. **circuitous**
   a. indirect, winding
   b. shaped like a circle
   c. confusing, baffling
   d. unusual, rare
   e. electrical circuits

2. **circulate**
   a. move in a restricted way
   b. use many words
   c. create controversy
   d. move continuously or freely
   e. explain carefully

3. **circumference**
   a. interior of a circle
   b. state of complete confusion
   c. volume of a circle
   d. area of a fence
   e. boundary of a circle

4. **circumlocution**
   a. area combining three intersections
   b. use of many words when fewer would suffice
   c. best form of locomotion
   d. combination of many items to create a whole
   e. last or largest train

5. **circumnavigate**
   a. sail into a storm
   b. become lost
   c. exaggerated an excuse
   d. dig around a hole
   e. sail all the way around

LESSON V: CIRCUM-, CONTRA-

6. **circumscribe**
   a. describe at length
   b. believe in
   c. draw a line or boundary around
   d. renew a subscription
   e. draw a two dimensional object

7. **circumspect**
   a. cautious
   b. unusual
   c. noticeable
   d. unexpected
   e. defeated

8. **circumstantial**
   a. coming to terms
   b. indicating fear
   c. pointing to a conclusion
   d. regarding weather
   e. going around

9. **circumvent**
   a. defeat
   b. destroy
   c. surround
   d. avoid
   e. cut off

10. **contraband**
    a. goods shipped within the U.S.
    b. illegally smuggled or imported goods
    c. confiscating illegal goods
    d. drugs made overseas
    e. banning drugs from export

11. **contraceptive**
    a. type of experimental medication
    b. device to induce pregnancy
    c. analgesic
    d. type of fertilizer
    e. device to prevent pregnancy

12. **contradict**
    a. smite
    b. agree
    c. say the opposite
    d. speak on someone's behalf
    e. prevent

13. **contrast**
    a. demerit
    b. striking similarity
    c. difference by comparison
    d. negative prediction
    e. shut away

14. **contravene**
    a. oppose
    b. mediate
    c. spy on
    d. speak against
    e. come together

15. **controversy**
    a. central act in a musical
    b. grape mixture in wine
    c. tone of apology
    d. heated disagreement
    e. faking of sincerity

LESSON V: CIRCUM-, CONTRA-

Exercise D

Solve the crossword puzzle.

Across
3. Longer than the most direct way, indirect. 5. To find a way around (an obstacle or problem). 7. To sail all the way around. 8. Serving to prevent pregnancy. 10. To differ strikingly. 11. Of no significance or incidental; dependent on circumstances. 12. To offend against the requirements (of a law, treaty, etc.); to oppose in argument. 13. Prolonged disagreement or heated debate. 14. To move or cause to move continuously or freely.

Down
1. The enclosing boundary of a circle. 2. The use of many words where fewer would do. 4. Cautious or prudent. 6. To deny the truth of (a statement) by asserting the opposite. 8. Goods that have been imported or exported illegally. 9. To restrict, limit; to draw a line around.

Lesson VI:
Co-, Col-, Com-, Con-, Cor-

CO-, COL- COM-, CON-, COR-
together

coalesce, coherent, collaborate, collateral, collision, collusion, commerce, commiserate, commission, composition, concoct, concord, condone, conference, congenital, consecrate, contrite, convene, correspondent, corroborate

Word Definitions

coalesce v. to come or bring together to form one mass or whole
"Many labor organizations and unions <u>coalesced</u> into the AFL-CIO."
coalescence (n.), coalescent (adj.)
coalescere to join, to grow together: *co-* together + *alescere* to grow up

coherent adj. (of an argument or theory) logical and consistent; holding together to form a whole
"He assembled his research notes into a <u>coherent</u> essay."
coherence (n.)
co- together + *haerrere* to stick

collaborate v. to work together on an activity or project
"I decided to <u>collaborate</u> with him, even though I was the better artist."
collaboration (n.)
collaborare to work with: *co-* together + *laborare* to work

collateral adj. accompanying as a subordinate
n. something pledged as security for repayment of a loan
"<u>Collateral</u> wartime damage refers to unintended civilian deaths."
collateralis collateral: *co-* together + *lateralis* lateral < *latus* side

LESSON VI: CO-, COL-, COM-, CON-, COR-

collision   **n.** the act or process of colliding; a crash or conflict
"A collision of views on immigration led to their disagreement."
collide (v.)
collidere to collide: *co-* together + *laedere* to strike

collusion   **n.** secret or illegal cooperation in order to cheat or to deceive others
"The price-fixing companies were found guilty of collusion."
collude (v.), collusive (adj.)
colludere to have a secret agreement: *co-* together + *ludere* to play

commerce   **n.** the activity of buying and selling
"The war ended all commerce between the countries."
commercium trade: *co-* together + *mercium* < *merx, mercis* merchandise

commiserate   **v.** to express sympathy or pity
"The girls commiserated after they were ignored by the same fickle boy."
commiserari to sympathize with: *co-* with + *miserari* to lament, to pity

commission   **n.** an instruction or command; a sum paid to an agent in a commercial transaction
v. to order or authorize the production of
"Michelangelo was commissioned to paint the Sistine Chapel."
committere to join, entrust: *co-* with + *mittere* to put or send

composition   **n.** the nature of the ingredients or constituents of a whole or mixture; a work of music, literature, or art
"Most of Chopin's works were compositions for piano."
componere to put together: *com-* together + *ponere* to put

concoct   **v.** to make (a dish or meal) by combining ingredients; to invent or devise (a story)
"The juvenile delinquents concocted a story about their whereabouts."
concoquere to cook by combining ingredients: *con-* together + *coquere* to cook

concord   **n.** an agreement; harmony; a treaty
"The once-warring factions finally achieved concord."
concordis of one mind, agreeing: *con-* together + *cor, cordis* heart, mind, spirit

condone   **v.** to accept or forgive (behavior considered wrong or offensive); to approve or sanction, especially reluctantly
"The teacher did not condone cheating of any kind."
condonare to make a present of; to forgive: *con-* together + *donare* to give

conference   **n.** a formal meeting of people with a shared interest
"A conference call involves multiple participants on the phone."
conferre to bring together: *con-* together + *ferre* to bring

congenital   **adj.** (especially of a diseases or abnormality) present from birth; present from the beginning
"An ailment you are born with is called congenital."
congenitus congenital: *con-* together + *genitus* born < *gignere* to beget

LESSON VI: CO-, COL-, COM-, CON-, COR-

consecrate   **v.** to make or declare sacred; to ordain to a sacred office
"The priest used holy water to consecrate the building."
consecration (n.)
consecrare to dedicate, to devote as sacred: *con-* together + *sacrare* to dedicate < *sacer* sacred

contrite   **adj.** feeling or expressing remorse
"The tearful lad apologized, feeling contrite about his mischief."
conterere to wear or grind down: *con-* with + *terere* to rub, to wear down

convene   **v.** to come or to bring together for a meeting or activity
"The Founding Fathers convened in Philadelphia."
convenire to assemble; to agree: *con-* together + *venire* to come

correspondent   **n.** a person who writes letters on a regular basis; a journalist reporting on a particular subject or from a particular place
"Edward Murrow was a radio correspondent in Europe in WWII."
correspondere to respond to: *co-* with + *respondere* to answer

corroborate   **v.** to confirm or lend support to (a statement or theory)
"An eyewitness corroborated the defendant's alibi."
corroboration (n.)
corroborare to reinforce: *co-* together + *roborare* to strengthen

EXERCISE A

Fill in the blanks in the sentences below with the correct form of a word in the scroll above.

1. Lucy McGillicutty's stories were never _____ because she often scrambled the beginning, middle, and end.

2. Judy made an appointment for a _____ with her chemistry teacher to go over the poor grade she received on her exam.

3. During WWII, my father was a _____ for "Newsweek".

4. Feeling _____ after abandoning her brother at home to go for ice cream with her friends, Jane brought home a double fudge sundae for him.

5. The Elks Society _____ at the lodge for conversation and supper.

6. In negotiations, the United States refuses to allow terrorists to use hostages as _____.

7. Sometimes a person with a _____ extra digit never knows of it, because it is removed shortly after birth.

LESSON VI:CO-, COL-, COM-, CON-, COR-

8. Although some environmental activists believe all nature was in a state of perfect _____ before the emergence of man, biologists agree the environment was in constant upheaval.

9. One can attribute Mozart's brilliance to his ability to create intricate _____ spontaneously.

10. The car's _____ with the tree was so loud we could hear it a block away.

11. The widows _____ over the loss of their husbands during the war.

12. The salesman's _____ put him over the top, and he won the best-of-the-year award.

13. The artist and author _____ to create a children's book with exceptional prose and illustrations.

14. Several of the boys were in _____ in a plot to destroy the school office.

15. His sister _____ his alibi, but their mother's account of events undermined it.

EXERCISE B

Match the word with the letter of its definition.

1. **coalesce**
2. **coherent**
3. **collaborate**
4. **collateral**
5. **collision**
6. **collusion**
7. **commerce**
8. **commiserate**
9. **commission**
10. **composition**
11. **concoct**
12. **concord**
13. **condone**
14. **conference**
15. **congenital**
16. **consecrate**
17. **contrite**
18. **convene**
19. **correspondent**
20. **corroborate**

a) create from lesser parts or ingredients
b) work of music, art, or literature
c) accept or forgive
d) give support to
e) trade or business
f) make sacred or holy
g) secret agreement to deceive others
h) work together on a project
i) formal meeting
j) come together to make a whole
k) feeling guilty
l) sympathize with the sorrow of another
m) logical and consistent
n) trait present from birth
o) harmony
p) security for a loan
q) crash
r) sum paid to an agent
s) person who writes letters on a regular basis
t) meet together

EXERCISE C

Circle the letter of the definition that best fits the meaning of the bold-faced word.

1. **coalesce**
   a. plan against
   b. allow to happen
   c. illustrate or write
   d. doubt
   e. come together to make a whole

2. **coherent**
   a. logical and consistent
   b. broken apart
   c. indirect and winding
   d. attached to
   e. depressing and hopeless

LESSON VI: CO-, COL-, COM-, CON-, COR-

3. **collaborate**
   a. be together on vacation
   b. work together
   c. study together
   d. explain carefully
   e. make up with different things

4. **collateral**
   a. sidewalk
   b. payment
   c. large amount of money
   d. guarantee on a loan
   e. stable period of the stock market

5. **collision**
   a. crash
   b. meal
   c. payment
   d. bush
   e. debate

6. **collusion**
   a. astute reference
   b. secret agreement
   c. violent meeting
   d. business referral
   e. molecular process

7. **commerce**
   a. adventure
   b. advertising
   c. trade
   d. meeting
   e. artwork

8. **commiserate**
   a. complain about
   b. make miserable
   c. give to another
   d. sympathize
   e. be similar to

9. **commission**
   a. bounty claimed
   b. sum paid to an agent
   c. purchase of a gift
   d. authorization
   e. piece of artwork

10. **composition**
    a. interjection
    b. creative work
    c. vessel
    d. trade
    e. excerpt

11. **concoct**
    a. sympathize with
    b. create an excerpt
    c. restore an antique
    d. make by combining parts
    e. siphon off slowly

12. **concord**
    a. disharmony
    b. substantial
    c. similar
    d. adjacent
    e. harmony

13. **condone**
    a. reprimand or punish
    b. accept or forgive
    c. make an agreement
    d. team up
    e. obey or comply

14. **conference**
    a. gathering among friends
    b. informal dinner party
    c. secret conversation
    d. formal meeting
    e. antique chair

15. **congenital**
    a. pensive thought
    b. trait present from birth
    c. disease
    d. genius
    e. mutation

16. **consecrate**
    a. make separate
    b. make public
    c. release tension
    d. bury
    e. make sacred

17. **contrite**
    a. short tempered
    b. feeling physical pain
    c. feeling guilt
    d. feeling lust
    e. feeling sadness

18. **convene**
    a. run into
    b. jump up
    c. herd animals
    d. call a meeting
    e. confer together

19. **correspondent**
    a. journalist
    b. despondent person
    c. regular waterworks
    d. textbook writer
    e. contrasting sweater

20. **corroborate**
    a. contribute to
    b. come together with
    c. be cheerful for
    d. give support to
    e. write a letter with

Exercise D

Solve the crossword puzzle.

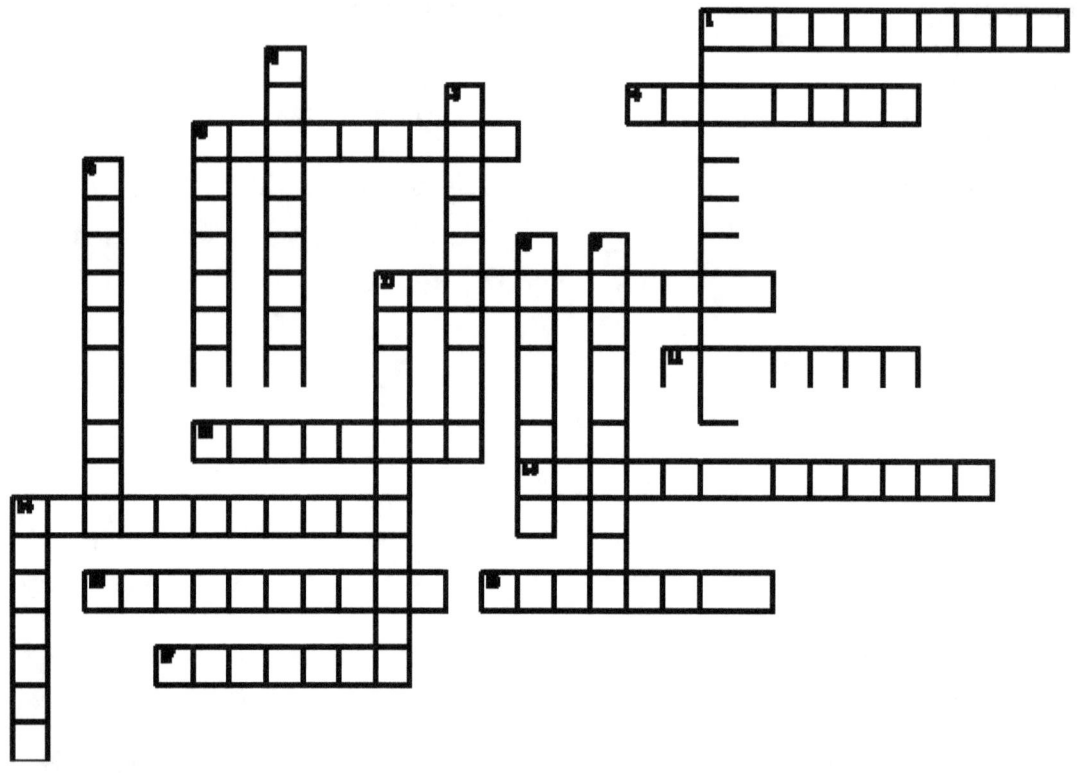

Across
1. An instrument or command; a sum paid to an agent in a commercial transaction. 4. The action of buying and selling, especially on a large scale. 5. A secret or illegal corporation in order to cheat or to deceive others. 10. To confirm or to give support to (a statement or theory). 11. To make (a dish or meal) by combining ingredients; to invent or devise (a story). 12. Feeling or expressing remorse. 13. A person who writes letters on a regular basis. 14. To work jointly on an activity or project. 15. (Especially of diseases or abnormalities) present from birth. 16. (Of an argument or theory) logical and consistent. 17. To accept or forgive (behavior considered wrong or offensive).

Down
1. The nature of the ingredients or constituents of a whole. 2. The act or process of colliding; a crash or conflict. 3. A formal meeting of people with a shared interest. 5. An agreement; harmony; a treaty. 6. Accompanying as a subordinate. 8. To come or bring together to form one mass or whole. 9. To make or declare sacred; to ordain to a sacred office. 10. To express sympathy or pity. 14. To come or to bring together for a meeting or activity.

Test 1

1. "Once a man has lost his self-respect, and has decided to <u>abjure</u> his better qualities and human dignity, he falls headlong, and cannot choose but do so."

   Poor Folk by Fyodor Dostoyevsky

   (a) forswear (b) proceed (c) prevent (d) precede (e) misuse

2. "For my part, I <u>abominate</u> all honorable respectable toils, trials, and tribulations of every kind whatsoever."

   Moby Dick by Herman Melville

   (a) cherish (b) detest (c) commit (d) choose (e) cause

3. "The ring-finger had suffered a slight <u>abrasion</u>, and the stain of the blood was still visible and unchanged after forty-one years."

   A Tramp Abroad by Mark Twain

   (a) discoloration (b) cut (c) breaking (d) scrape
   (e) mistreatment

4. "And next, I was <u>abstemious</u> because my way led among books and students where no drinking was."

   John Barleycorn by Jack London

   (a) hurriedly leaving (b) bringing a change (c) having mixed feelings
   (d) eating and drinking in moderation (e) exercising to excess

5. "He had read a great deal, chiefly delighting in books, which were unusual; and he poured forth his stores of <u>abstruse</u> knowledge with child-like enjoyment of the amazement of his hearers."

   Of Human Bondage by Somerset Maugham

   (a) complex (b) antiquated (c) insufficient (d) concise (e) compounded

6. "Had he imposed on a child, I should have been more <u>averse</u> to have forgiven him; but a woman upwards of thirty must certainly be supposed to know what will make her most happy."

   Tom Jones by Henry Fielding

   (a) carefully placed (b) strongly disinclined (c) easily corrupted
   (d) conveniently indisposed (e) occasionally connected

7. "Standing on a projecting rock, he played several tunes in the hope that the fish, attracted by his melody, would of their own accord dance into his net, which he had placed below."

Fables by Aesop

    (a) occupation   (b) agreement   (c) collection   (d) reward
    (e) good will

8. "The old count began irresolutely to admonish Nicholas and beg him to abandon his purpose."

War and Peace by Leo Tolstoy

    (a) avoid   (b) restrict   (c) reprimand   (d) forgive   (e) corrupt

9. "The Oregon [matter] and the annexation of Texas are now all-important to the security and future peace and prosperity of our union...."

Letter, March 5, 1844 by U.S. President Andrew Jackson

    (a) attachment   (b) movement   (c) creation   (d) declaration
    (e) holy place

10. "The new art takes the monument where it finds it, incrusts itself there, assimilates it to itself, develops it according to its fancy, and finishes it if it can."

Notre-Dame de Paris by Victor Hugo

    (a) points and occupies   (b) makes it sacred   (c) borrows from
    (d) pays a sum   (e) incorporates

11. "Her face was the oddest mixture of youth and maturity, and beneath her candid brow her searching little smile seemed to contain a world of ambiguous intentions."

The American by Henry James

    (a) guilty   (b) unclear   (c) left or right handed
    (d) constantly moving   (e) opposite

12. "The lakes are something which you are unprepared for; they lie up so high, exposed to the light, and the forest is diminished to a fine fringe on their edges, with here and there a blue mountain, like amethyst jewels set around some jewel of the first water - so anterior, so superior, to all the changes that are to take place on their shores, even now civil and refined, and fair as they can ever be."

"Ktaddn" from *The Maine Woods* by Henry David Thoreau

    (a) preexisting   (b) simultaneously   (c) later   (d) before noon
    (e) after noon

13. "Interpreting Hester Prynne's deportment as an appeal of this nature, society was inclined to show its former victim a more benign countenance than she cared to be favoured with, or, perchance, than she deserved."

    The Scarlet Letter by Nathaniel Hawthorne

    (a) Judgmental (b) harmless (c) malignant (d) reasonable (e) unimpressive

14. "This valley bifurcates to the parallel of the Antilles, and terminates at the mouth by the enormous depression of 9,000 yards."

    20,000 Leagues Under The Sea by Jules Verne

    (a) complicates   (b) opposes   (c) divides into two   (d) disagrees
    (e) severely restricts

15. "As the president finished reading the paper (which I beg leave to assure my readers is a bonafide copy of one written by bonafide girls once upon a time), a round of applause followed.."

    Little Women by Louisa May Alcott

    (a) false   (b) artificial   (c) authentic   (d) spurious   (e) faithful

16. "By taking a circuitous route, and, as it appeared to her, very unreasonable direction to the knoll, they were soon beyond her eye; and for some minutes longer she remained without sight or sound of any companion."

    Mansfield Park by Jane Austen

    (a) circular   (b) indirect   (c) lengthy   (d) erroneous   (e) flexible

17. "Take care, however, you don't betray either of us to Zoraide--to my daughter, I mean; she is so discreet and circumspect herself, she cannot understand that one should find a pleasure in gossiping a little."

    The Professor by Charlotte Bronte

    (a) unwise   (b) restrictive (c) prudent   (d) doubtful   (e) entertaining

18. "Her skin was brown, her eyes certainly brighter, and she attended to what was said as though she might be going to contradict it."

    The Voyage Out by Virginia Woolf

    (a) give support   (b) prevent advancement   (c) trying to control
    (d) look into   (e) say the opposite

19. "It would have been to <u>contravene</u> these arrangements if Rosamond had consented to go away to Stone Court or elsewhere, as her parents wished her to do."
    Middlemarch by George Eliot

    (a) support   (b) establish   (c) absorb   (d) agree with   (e) violate

20. "At the time of our visit, there were four chiefs in arms contending for supremacy in the government: if one succeeded in becoming for a time very powerful, the others <u>coalesced</u> against him; but no sooner were they victorious, than they were again hostile to each other."
    The Voyage of the Beagle by Charles Darwin

    (a) misused   (b) bound together   (c) canceled   (d) supported   (e) pulled apart

21. "He is liable for direct damage both to your chimneys and any <u>collateral</u> damage caused by fall of bricks into garden, etc."
    Actions and Reactions by Rudyard Kipling

    (a) coinciding   (b) cautious   (c) colliding   (d) concocting   (e) combining

22. "There was <u>collusion</u>, sir, or that villain never would have escaped."
    Vanity Fair by William Makepeace Thackeray

    (a) avoidance   (b) dangerous device   (c) secret agreement   (d) harmonious visitation   (e) hostility

23. "As was the custom, she usually accompanied her parents to church on Sunday afternoons; but Mrs. Welland <u>condoned</u> her truancy, having that very morning won her over to the necessity of a long engagement.."
    The Age of Innocence by Edith Wharton

    (a) avoided   (b) limited   (c) disagreed with   (d) prevented   (e) forgave

24. "Both Kristoforas and his brother, Juozapas, were cripples, the latter having lost one leg by having it run over, and Kristoforas having <u>congenital</u> dislocation of the hip, which made it impossible for him ever to walk."
    The Jungle by Upton Sinclair

    (a) inherited   (b) sympathy towards   (c) present at birth   (d) infectious   (e) avoided arrest

25. "There are many physical as well as moral facts which <u>corroborate</u> this opinion, and some few that would seem to weigh against it."
    The Last of The Mohicans by James Fenimore Cooper

    (a) harmonize   (b) conform   (c) disagree with   (d) support   (e) cancel

Lesson VII:
De-

DE-
down, from, about

debase, decadence, deciduous, dedicate, deflation, demented, demolish, demote, depend, dependent, depreciate, descendant, describe, desiccate, despise, despondent, deter, deviate, devious, devour

Word Definitions

debase
v. to lower the quality, value, or character of
"The nasty remarks were intended to <u>debase</u> the woman's virtue."
debasement (n.)
de- down from + *base* base or pedestal

decadence
n. the process or manifestation of moral, physical or cultural decline
"Drunkenness, lewd behavior, and cursing are signs of his <u>decadence</u>."
de- from + *cadere* to fall

deciduous
adj. (of a tree or shrub) shedding its leaves annually
"Oaks and other hardwoods are <u>deciduous</u>, while pines are coniferous."
decidere to detach, to cut off: *de-* from + *cidere* (variant of *caedere*) to cut

dedicate
v. to devote to a subject, task, or purpose; to address a book or composition to someone as a sign of respect or affection
"A professional musician <u>dedicates</u> most of his time to practice."
dedicare to devote, to declare: *de-* about + *dicare* to devote

deflation
n. the action or process of releasing gas from something; diminishment in importance; decrease in prices
"The tennis player's high hopes for victory suffered <u>deflation</u> when he lost the set."
de- (expressing reversal) + *flare* to blow, to breathe

demented	**adj.** insane; wild and irrational; suffering from dementia "The patient believed he was rational, but he was clearly <u>demented</u>." *demens, dementis* insane: *de-* from + *mens, mentis* mind, reason
demolish	**v.** to knock down (a building); to refute or to defeat "The clever debater <u>demolished</u> his opponent's argument." *demolition (n.)* *demoliri* to remove, tear down: *de-* (expressing reversal) + *moliri* to build, to labor at
demote	**v.** to revoke a higher rank or senior position "The disobedient corporal was <u>demoted</u> to the rank of private." *demotion (n.)* *de-* down + *movere* to move
depend	**v.** to be controlled or determined by; to rely on "Edison said invention <u>depends</u> more on perspiration than inspiration." *dependent (adj.)* *dependere* to depend, to hang down from: *de-* down + *pendere* to hang
dependent	**n.** a person who relies on another, especially a family member, for financial support "Children under 18 are considered legal <u>dependents</u> of their parents." *dependere* to depend, to hang down from: *de-* down + *pendere* to hang
depreciate	**v.** to diminish in value over a period of time; to disparage or belittle "New cars <u>depreciate</u> rapidly in value; land values tend to appreciate." *depreciare* to lower in price, to undervalue: *de-* down + *pretium* price
descendant	**n.** a person or animal that is descended from a particular ancestor "*Homo sapiens* and apes are <u>descendants</u> of a common ancestor." *descendere* to descend, to climb down: *de-* down + *scandere* to climb
describe	**v.** to give a detailed account of (someone or something) "Dickens <u>describes</u> his characters so well that readers feel they know them." *describere* to describe, to copy: *de-* down + *scribere* to write
desiccate	**v.** to remove the moisture from "Mummies lasted because their tissues were <u>desiccated</u> before burial." *desiccation (n.)* *desiccare* to make thoroughly dry: *de-* about + *siccare* to dry, to drain
despise	**v.** to feel contempt or disrespect for "As a child I <u>despised</u> spinach, but now I enjoy the taste of it." *despicere* to look down on, to despise: *de-* down + *spicere* to look at
despondent	**adj.** in low spirits (from loss of hope) "The child was <u>despondent</u> at the death of her dog." *despondere* to give up, to abandon: *de-* away + *spondere* to promise

deter	v. to discourage (someone) from doing something by instilling fear of the consequences
"The snowstorm deterred us from attending the party."
deterrere to scare away, to discourage: *de-* away + *terrere* to scare

deviate	v. to diverge from an established course or from usual or accepted standards
n. one who varies markedly from the norm; a deviant
"The reckless driver deviated from the proper lane."
deviare to turn out of the way: *de-* away + *via* road, way

devious	adj. skillfully using underhand tactics to achieve goals; (of a route or journey) indirect, or twisting and turning
"Foxes are portrayed in fables as devious, chickens as stupid."
devius remote, devious: *de-* away + *via* road, way

devour	v. to eat voraciously or quickly
"After going without food for three days, the rescued man devoured the dinner."
devorare to devour, to consume: *de-* down + *vorare* to swallow

EXERCISE A

Fill in the blanks in the sentences below with the correct form of a word in the scroll above.

1. Legend has it that no man or machine can ever _____ Stonehenge, for it is protected by Merlin himself.

2. Brad was distraught when he discovered that his gluttonous friends had _____ all of Jennifer's famous chocolate chip cookies.

3. Helen wondered if Jack Nicholson was perhaps _____ himself after watching his stunning portrayals of madmen in *One Flew Over the Cuckoo's Nest* and *The Shining*.

4. Private Ryan was once a major, but he was _____ after a case of liquor was found in his locker.

5. Britney used to travel to New England every autumn to view the brilliant foliage on the _____ trees along the highways and byways.

6. During the Great Depression, people did not want their bonds to _____, so they took their money out of banks and hid cash under their mattresses.

7. In the old West, criminals would be put on display so that the townspeople could _____ them publicly.

LESSON VII: DE-

8. Johnny allowed his fear of heights to _____ him from trying rock climbing.

9. Angry about their exclusion from the varsity lacrosse team, James and John formulated a _____ plan to infect the entire team with chicken pox.

10. At the time of their divorce, the couple did not think it possible to _____ one another to any greater extent.

11. Enrique _____ from the path and became lost in the woods.

12. After thinking about the intruder's appearance, the witness was able to fully _____ him.

13. George W. Bush is a _____ of former U.S. President George H.W. Bush.

14. Raisins are basically _____ grapes.

15. Of the family's three children, only the youngest one is still a _____.

16. The _____ of the kingdom was most obvious at holiday celebrations, when the royals ate and drank to excess.

17. After a tornado destroyed the Parkers' house, they became _____.

18. Children _____ on their parents until they are fully grown.

19. The _____ of a zeppelin takes several hours because the hydrogen must be let out slowly to maintain safety.

20. The graduating class _____ the yearbook to Mr. Bragdon, the retiring headmaster.

EXERCISE B

Match the word with the letter of its definition.

1. debase
2. decadence
3. deciduous
4. dedicate
5. deflation
6. demented
7. demolish
8. demote
9. depend
10. dependent
11. depreciate
12. descendant
13. describe
14. desiccate
15. despise
16. despondent
17. deter
18. deviate
19. devious
20. devour

a) discourage; prevent from occurring
b) person who relies on another
c) lower in rank or grade
d) not straightforward; full of tricks
e) mentally ill, disturbed
f) consume with great vigor
g) person of specific lineage
h) remove moisture from
i) having no hope; greatly depressed
j) decrease in value
k) shedding leaves each year
l) destroy; tear down
m) process of moral or cultural decline
n) address a book to a person
o) action of air leaving a chamber
p) consider beneath oneself
q) give a detailed account
r) turn off course
s) rely on
t) lower the quality, value, or character of

EXERCISE C

Circle the letter of the definition that best fits the meaning of the bold-faced word.

1. **debase**
   a. climb down a mountain
   b. raise the temperature of
   c. reject the choice of
   d. lower the quality, value, or character of
   e. choose an alternate or substitute

2. **decadence**
   a. process of moral or cultural decline
   b. musical phrase
   c. falling of leaves
   d. suffering from dementia
   e. calling of doves

3. **deciduous**
   a. pertaining to farming
   b. decaying of compost
   c. shedding leaves each year
   d. inscribing a message
   e. blowing air in a balloon

4. **dedicate**
   a. use up
   b. consume
   c. take advantage
   d. devote to a purpose
   e. set aside

5. **deflation**
   a. blowing up a balloon
   b. air leaving a chamber
   c. filling up a chamber
   d. draining a swimming pool
   e. taking in knowledge

6. **demented**
   a. mentally stable
   b. narcissistic
   c. suspicious
   d. irrational
   e. confused

7. **demolish**
   a. rebuild
   b. destroy
   c. build up
   d. consume
   e. sacrifice

8. **demote**
   a. lower in rank or grade
   b. give a raise
   c. admonish or impugn
   d. praise or cheer
   e. punish or reprimand

9. **depend**
   a. deflate
   b. suffer
   c. rely on
   d. devalue
   e. knock down

10. **dependent**
    a. controlled substance
    b. person who relies on another
    c. poor person
    d. person who eats with someone
    e. lower rank

11. **depreciate**
    a. increase in value
    b. conserve value
    c. save money
    d. decrease in value
    e. spend money

LESSON VII: DE-

12. **descendant**
    a. steep decline
    b. person of a specific lineage
    c. rocky hill
    d. person born a foreigner
    e. person of questionable heritage

13. **describe**
    a. give a detailed account
    b. handle with great care
    c. change sides in a game
    d. give away everything
    e. come home empty-handed

14. **desiccate**
    a. hydrate quickly
    b. lift off
    c. remove moisture from
    d. give a detailed account
    e. discourage

15. **despise**
    a. spy on
    b. say the opposite of
    c. demolish
    d. feel contempt for
    e. rely on

16. **despondent**
    a. reliant on others
    b. playful
    c. having no hope
    d. demented
    e. having good cheer

17. **deter**
    a. discourage from doing
    b. set an appointment
    c. avoid
    d. throw at
    e. help out

18. **deviate**
    a. put aside
    b. turn off course
    c. stay on track
    d. bend over
    e. turn around

19. **devious**
    a. full of tricks
    b. overt
    c. full of spite
    d. truthful
    e. off-beat

20. **devour**
    a. eat delicately
    b. to climb
    c. to eat with vigor
    d. to jump down
    e. to eat slowly

Exercise D

Solve the crossword puzzle.

Across
1. A person who relies on another for financial support. 2. To diverge from an established course or accepted standards. 4. To devote to a subject, task, or purpose; to address a book to a person. 6. To discourage (someone) from doing something by instilling fear of the consequences. 7. A person or animal that is descended from a particular ancestor. 12. To lower the quality, value, or character of. 13. (Of a tree or shrub) shedding its leaves annually. 15. To diminish in value over a period of time; to disparage or belittle. 16. The process or manifestation of moral, physical or cultural decline.

Down
1. The action or process of releasing gas from or being diminished in importance. 3. In low spirits from loss of hope or courage. 5. To be controlled or determined by; to rely on. 6. Skillfully using underhand tactics to achieve goals. 7. Wild and irrational; suffering from dementia. 8. To give a lower rank or less senior position to. 9. To remove the moisture from. 10. To eat voraciously or quickly. 11. To feel contempt for. 14. To knock down (a building); to refute or defeat. 15. To give a detailed account of (someone or something).

Lesson VIII:
Dis-, Duo-

DIS-
away from, apart

DUO-
two

diffident, dilapidated, discern, discontent, discord, discredit, discrepancy, disintegrate, dispel, dissent, dissident, distortion, distract, diverge, dual, duet, duo, duplex, duplicate, duplicity

Word Definitions

diffident **adj.** modest or shy because of a lack of self confidence "You can get this job: Just don't be <u>diffident</u> in the interview."
diffidence (n.)
diffidere to distrust, to lack confidence: *dis-* away from + *fidere* trust

dilapidated **adj.** in a state of disrepair or ruin as a result of age or neglect
"Poor inner city people often live in crumbling, <u>dilapidated</u> housing."
dilapidation (n.)
dilapidare to demolish, to scatter: *dis-* apart + *lapidare* to throw stones < *lapis, lapidis* stone

discern **v.** to see or understand (an object or pattern); to distinguish mentally (from something else)
"He could barely <u>discern</u> the cottage in the fog."
discernere to see, to distinguish: *dis-* apart + *cernere* to separate

discontent **n.** a lack of contentment or satisfaction
"Lack of adequate food can lead to popular <u>discontent</u>."
discontentment (n.)
dis- away from + *contentus* satisfied

LESSON VIII: DIS-, DUO-

discord
n. a lack of agreement or harmony
"The abortion question has led to grave political discord."
discordare to quarrel < *discors* disagreeing: *dis-* apart + *cor, cordis* heart, mind, spirit

discredit
v. to harm the good reputation of; to show the incorrectness of (an idea)
n. a loss or lack of reputation
"To his discredit, the honor student was discovered cheating."
dis- away from + *credere* to believe, to trust

discrepancy
n. an inconsistency between two or more facts, ideas or things
"There's often a discrepancy between promise and delivery."
discrepant (adj.)
discrepare to disagree, to dispute: *dis-* away from + *crepare* to crack

disintegrate
v. to break into small parts as a result of impact or decay; to lose strength and gradually fail
"Good health tends to disintegrate with old age."
dis- (expressing reversal) + *integrare* to make whole

dispel
v. to make (a feeling or belief) disappear
"His safe arrival dispelled the rumor of his death."
dispellere to drive apart: *dis-* (expressing intensity) + *pellere* to drive out

dissent
v. to express disagreement with a prevailing view or official decision
n. the holding of or expression of a dissenting view
"A true democracy welcomes dissent from the majority opinion."
dissentire to disagree, to differ: *dis-* apart + *sentire* feel or think

dissident
n. a person who opposes official policy
"Many of the colonists were dissidents who protested British rule."
dissidere to disagree, to be separated: *dis-* apart + *sidere* sit

distortion
n. the act of twisting (something) out of shape; an untruthful or unfair representation (of something)
"A funhouse mirror causes elongation and distortion of features."
distorquere to twist apart: *dis-* apart + *torquere* turn or twist

distract
v. to prevent (someone) from concentrating on something
"I went to a movie to distract me from my sorrow."
distrahere to draw apart: *dis-* apart + *trahere* to draw or drag

diverge
v. (of a road, line, or idea) to separate and go in a different direction; to depart from (a set course or standard)
"We usually agree, but our opinions diverge on this subject."
divergere to diverge: *dis-* apart + *vergere* to turn or incline

dual
adj. consisting of two parts, elements, or aspects
"The nose has a dual purpose: to breathe and smell."
dualize (v.)
duo two

LESSON VIII: DIS-, DUO-

duet	**n.** a performance by two singers, instrumentalists, or dancers "In the opera, the hero and heroine sing a <u>duet</u>." *duo* two
duo	**n.** a pair of people or things "Batman and Robin are known as the 'dynamic duo.'" *duo* two
duplex	**n.** a residential building divided into two apartments "Two homes adjoining in a single building constitute a <u>duplex</u>." *duplicare* to double: *duo-* two + *plicare* to fold
duplicate	**v.** to make an exact copy of; to do again unnecessarily **n.** an exact copy **adj.** exactly like something else; having two corresponding parts "No one can <u>duplicate</u> the artistry of Leonardo da Vinci." *duplicable/duplicative (adj.)* *duplicare* to double: *duo-* two + *plicare* to fold
duplicity	**n.** deceitfulness; untruth through deception; two-facedness "Disguise, trickery, and misinformation are forms of <u>duplicity</u>." *duplicare* to double: *duo-* two + *plicare* to fold

EXERCISE A.

Fill in the blanks in the sentences below with the correct form of a word in the scroll above.

1. The tourists grew apprehensive at the sight of so many _____ buildings as they traveled through the city.

2. Macbeth could not _____ the dread and consternation that seized him when he saw Banquo's ghost.

3. Forrest Gump, _____ in his early years, surprised those who knew him with his later success and self-assurance.

4. Without peace there will be _____ in the world.

5. The _____ objective of the restoration was to make the house safe for its inhabitants and to achieve historic preservation status.

6. The Roman Empire, attacked by barbarians from without and divided by rancorous factions from within, _____.

7. Good writers do not let the temptations of e-mail and the telephone _____ them from their work.

LESSON VIII: DIS-, DUO-

8. Although he once believed he owned the original Mona Lisa, Mr. Thomson was embarrassed to find that his painting was only a _____ .

9. Martha Stuart's explanation of a suspiciously timed stock trade was _____ by phone records and other witnesses' testimony.

10. Salvador Dali's _____ of ordinary objects, such as melting watches, is a hallmark of his surrealist paintings.

11. The concert concluded with a _____ performed by the two famous violinists.

12. After the controversial law passed the Legislature, many citizens rallied to express their _____

13. The sight of an imperial officer lying on the deck in a breathless and quivering heap caused other would-be _____ to think twice about rebelling openly against Darth Vader.

14. Her philandering husband's _____ stunned Maryanne.

15. I was forced to decide whether to go left or right when the two roads _____ in the wood.

16. When Julius Caesar extended his hand in greeting, he did not _____ the dagger concealed in Brutus' left hand.

17. The young couple lived on the second floor of a _____ until they could afford a single-family home.

18. The _____ between Hamlet's outward appearance of madness and inward lucidity leads the audience to conclude that he is pretending insanity.

19. The students expressed their _____ with the cafeteria food.

20. The "dynamic _____" were famous as cartoon characters as well as movie stars.

EXERCISE B

Match the word with the letter of its definition.

1. **diffident**
2. **dilapidated**
3. **discern**
4. **discontent**
5. **discord**
6. **discredit**
7. **discrepancy**
8. **disintegrate**
9. **dispel**
10. **dissent**
11. **dissident**
12. **distortion**
13. **distract**
14. **diverge**
15. **dual**
16. **duet**
17. **duo**
18. **duplex**
19. **duplicate**
20. **duplicity**

a) person who disagrees (with a policy)
b) consisting of two parts, elements, or aspects
c) action of changing shape or appearance
d) express disagreement
e) reserved, shy
f) make an exact copy
g) pair of people or things
h) drive away
i) dissatisfaction
j) perceive
k) state of disagreement
l) break apart into small pieces
m) in ruin, falling apart
n) harm the reputation of
o) inconsistency
p) draw attention away from
q) deceitfulness
r) residential building divided into two apartments
s) go off in different directions
t) performance by two singers, instrumentalists, or dancers

EXERCISE C

Circle the letter of the definition that best fits the meaning of the bold-faced word.

1. **diffident**
   a. haughty; aloof
   b. proper; polite
   c. callous; uncaring
   d. reserved; shy
   e. hopeless; depressed

2. **dilapidated**
   a. ancient
   b. pathetic
   c. in ruin; falling apart
   d. dirty; disgusting
   e. unworthy of consideration

3. **discern**
   a. copy
   b. perceive
   c. determine
   d. pay attention
   e. confuse

4. **discontent**
   a. state of disagreement
   b. destructive turn of events
   c. civil unrest
   d. fury over an affair
   e. dissatisfaction with circumstances

5. **discord**
   a. state of satisfaction
   b. inconsistency
   c. dissatisfaction with circumstances
   d. state of disagreement
   e. state of confusion

6. **discredit**
   a. cause distress
   b. harm the reputation of
   c. owe a debt
   d. lose a battle
   e. balance an account

7. **discrepancy**
   a. error
   b. loss of respect
   c. state of disagreement
   d. instance of inconsistency
   e. dissatisfaction

8. **disintegrate**
   a. go off in different directions
   b. remove from a whole
   c. cast off; ignore
   d. break into small pieces
   e. build up

9. **dispel**
   a. relate to others
   b. drive away
   c. cast a spell
   d. come together
   e. draw attention

10. **dissent**
    a. deem noble
    b. treat with disdain
    c. plot to destroy
    d. express disagreement
    e. fall down

11. **dissident**
    a. false memory
    b. inconsistency
    c. person of great importance
    d. disagreement
    e. person who disagrees

12. **distortion**
    a. loud sound
    b. intense dislike
    c. misrepresentation
    d. increase
    e. falsehood

LESSON VIII: DIS-, DUO-

13. distract
   a. blend in
   b. deceive
   c. go off in different directions
   d. confuse
   e. draw attention away

14. diverge
   a. drive away
   b. attract attention
   c. confuse
   d. disagree
   e. go off in a different direction

15. dual
   a. pertaining to three elements
   b. consisting of two parts
   c. disagreeing
   d. coming together
   e. a sword fight

16. duet
   a. dissatisfaction among performers
   b. concert
   c. changing shape
   d. performance of two performers
   e. disagreement between two friends

17. duo
   a. single person or thing
   b. piano performance
   c. pair of people or things
   d. concerto
   e. trio of animals

18. duplex
   a. commercial building with apartments
   b. community center
   c. school playground
   d. high-rise building
   e. residential building divided into two apartments

19. duplicate
   a. make an exact copy
   b. create a copy machine
   c. pair up people
   d. perform twice
   e. draw attention

20. duplicity
   a. cheerfulness
   b. hopelessness
   c. deceitfulness
   d. happiness
   e. calmness

Exercise D

Solve the crossword puzzle.

Across
7. To make (a feeling or belief) disappear. 8. A twisting out of shape; an untruthful or unfair representation. 10. To recognize or find out. 11. To make an exact copy of; to do again unnecessarily. 12. A performance by two singers, instrumentalists, or dancers. 13. To harm the good reputation of. 15. Consisting of two parts, elements, or aspects. 16. A lack of contentment or satisfaction.

Down
1. In a state of disrepair or ruin as a result of age or neglect. 2. An inconsistency between two things or ideas. 3. Deceitfulness. 4. To express disagreement with a prevailing view or decision. 5. (Of a road, course or line) to separate and go in a different direction. 6. To fall apart; to lose strength and gradually fail. 7. A person who opposes official policy. 9. To prevent (someone) from concentrating. 12. A lack of agreement or harmony. 13. A residential building divided into two apartments. 14. A pair of people or things. 15. Modest or shy.

Lesson IX:
Ex-, Equi-, Extra-

EX-
out, from

EQUI-
equal

EXTRA-
beyond, outside

*equilateral, equilibrium, equity, equivalent,
elaborate, emigrate, eminent, enervate, eradicate, erosion, evoke,
excise, exclusive, exhilarate, exonerate, exorbitant,
extracurricular, extraneous, extravagant, extrovert*

Word Definitions

elaborate
v. to develop or present in further detail
adj. involving many carefully arranged parts; detailed and complicated
"The president said no more; he did not elaborate on his statement."
elaboration (n.)
elaborare to work out: *ex-* out + *laborare* to work

emigrate
v. to leave one's native country to reside in another
"The Irish emigrated from their homeland to escape the potato famine."
emigration (n.), emigrant (n.)
emigrare to emigrate: *ex-* out + *migrare* to move

eminent
adj. distinguished within a particular sphere;
notable "The Pope is more eminent than an
archbishop." *eminere* to jut, to project: *ex-* out +
minere push

enervate
v. to cause to feel drained of energy
"The runner felt utterly enervated after running the marathon."
enervation (n.)
enervare to weaken: *ex-* out + *nervus, nervi* muscle, strength

LESSON IX: EX-, EQUI-, EXTRA-

eradicate   **v.** to remove or destroy completely
"Smallpox was <u>eradicated</u> in the U.S. several decades ago."
eradication (n.)
eradicare to tear up by the roots: *ex-* out + *radicare* to take root

erosion   **n.** the process or result of gradually wearing away
"The sandy beach was created by millennia of <u>erosion</u> from the force of the waves crushing rocks and shells."
erosive (adj.), erode (v.)
ex- away + *rodere* to gnaw

evoke   **v.** to bring or recall to the conscious mind
"A tea-soaked cake <u>evoked</u> a torrent of memory in Proust."
evocation (n.)
evocare to call forth: *ex-* out of + *vocare* to call

excise   **v.** to cut out surgically; to remove from a text or piece of music
n. an internal tax on produced goods
"The surgeon <u>excised</u> the bullet from the soldier's thigh."
excision (n.)
excidere to cut out: *ex-* out + *caedere* to cut

exclusive   **adj.** excluding or not admitting other things; restricted to the person, group, or area concerned; high-class
"The <u>exclusive</u> golf club accepted only millionaires as members."
excludere to shut out, remove: *ex-* out + *claudere* to shut

exhilarate   **v.** to make very happy or animated
"She was <u>exhilarated</u> to learn she had been accepted to Princeton."
exhilaration (n.)
exhilarare to gladden: *ex-* (expressing emphasis) + *hilaris* cheerful

exonerate   **v.** to absolve from blame
"The suspect was freed after being <u>exonerated</u> by a DNA test."
exoneration (n.), exonerative (adj.)
exonerare to free from a burden: *ex-* out + *onerare* to burden

exorbitant   **adj.** (of a price or amount) unreasonably high
"The Hummer comes with an <u>exorbitant</u> price tag."
exorbitare to derail: *ex-* out + *orbita* wheel-track or rut

equilateral   **adj.** having all its sides of the same length
"The facade of an A-frame house has <u>equilateral</u> sides."
aequilaterus equal-sided: *aequi-* equal + *laterus* of sides

equilibrium   **n.** a state in which opposing forces or influences are balanced; a calm state of mind
"Wild gains and losses are eventually leveled in a market <u>equilibrium</u>."
aequilibrium level (position of scales): *aequi-* equal + *libra* scales

LESSON IX: EX-, EQUI-, EXTRA-

equity n. fairness and impartiality; the value of shares issued by a company; value of a property or asset minus any debts against it
"The judge was known for his equity in commercial disputes."
aequitas justice, impartiality < *equus* equal

equivalent adj. equal or nearly equal in value, amount, function, or meaning
"100 degrees Celsius and 212 degrees Fahrenheit are equivalent." *equivalence (n.)*
aequivalere to be of equal worth or power: *aequi-* equal + *valere* to be strong, to prevail

extracurricular adj. (of a school-related activity) pursued in addition to the main curriculum
"Optional activities like orchestra and football are considered extracurricular."
extra- outside + *curriculum* course or racing chariot

extraneous adj. irrelevant or unrelated to the subject
"Many algebra word problems contain extraneous information that confuses the test taker."
extraneus external, foreign: *extra-* outside + *-ous*

extravagant adj. lacking restraint in spending money or using resources; exceeding what is reasonable or appropriate
"Paying $100 for a single bottle of wine seems extravagant."
extravagance (n.)
extravagare to wander or roam: *extra-* outside + *vagare* to wander

extrovert n. an outgoing, socially confident person
"Cheerleaders typically are extroverts." *extroversion (n.)*, *extroverted (adj.)* *extra-* outside + *vertere* to turn

EXERCISE A

Fill in the blanks in the sentences below with the correct form of a word in the scroll above.

1. Kozlowski threw _____ parties to show off his wealth.

2. The Dave Matthews Band _____ audiences with its stunning passion and electric virtuosity, always leaving them demanding more.

3. Although the executive aspired to drive a Lamborghini, he knew the car's _____ price tag would ruin his budget.

4. Tupac Shakur, The Notorious B.I.G., and other _____ rappers are remembered as much for their violent deaths as for their musical contributions.

LESSON IX: EX-, EQUI-, EXTRA-

5. An _____ triangle has three identical sides.

6. Although yellow fever has been _____ in the United States, it still exists in countries unable to properly vaccinate against it.

7. Shakespeare's plays can be incredibly long when performed, but many acting companies would consider it heresy to _____ a single passage for the sake of brevity.

8. Although he was acquitted of murder, no amount of evidence will ever _____ O. J. Simpson in the court of public opinion.

9. The value of the _____ usually exceeds the value of the bonds.

10. Tourists find themselves so awed by the size of the Colisseum, they often forget to consider how _____ the architectural design was for the time.

11. You would think that all professional actors are _____ by nature, but in fact many of them are quite reserved off camera.

12. Since the issue has been settled, any further debate would be _____.

13. When two formulas express the same value, they are _____.

14. The sweltering climate of the Florida Everglades _____ even the most ardent collectors of the rare orchids that grow there.

15. Steven hoped that his diverse _____ activities (he was captain of the lacrosse team, editor of the student paper, and class president) would make up for his lackluster test scores when he applied to colleges.

16. Lo-Han's parents _____ from China while in their teens.

17. The flow of water downhill carved a channel in the rocks after thousands of years of _____.

18. When the titration was completed and the solution was neither acidic or basic, it was at _____.

19. Carrot Top could not _____ laughter from an audience, even if he were to run around in clown shoes with his pants on fire.

20. Puff Daddy's parties are very _____; his old friends aren't invited, and instead the guest list reads like a *Who's Who* of Hollywood.

LESSON IX: EX-, EQUI-, EXTRA-

EXERCISE B

Match the word with the letter of its definition.

1. **elaborate**
2. **emigrate**
3. **eminent**
4. **enervate**
5. **equilateral**
6. **equilibrium**
7. **equity**
8. **equivalent**
9. **eradicate**
10. **erosion**
11. **evoke**
12. **excise**
13. **exclusive**
14. **exhilarate**
15. **exonerate**
16. **exorbitant**
17. **extracurricular**
18. **extraneous**
19. **extravagant**
20. **extrovert**

a) beyond what is reasonable
b) get rid of entirely
c) spending carelessly or lavishly
d) gradual process of wear
e) equal in value, amount, etc.
f) calm state
g) detailed and complicated
h) shutting out all or most others
i) prominent or distinguished
j) prove or declare innocent
k) call forth
l) outside regular course of study
m) sap vigor or strength
n) cut out; remove
o) leave one's country for another
p) make lively
q) unessential, peripheral
r) person who readily shares feelings
s) value of shares issued by a company
t) having all its sides of the same length

EXERCISE C

Circle the letter of the definition that best fits the meaning of the bold-faced word.

1. **elaborate**
    a. prominent or distinguished
    b. sophisticated; high class
    c. having good intentions
    d. detailed or complicated
    e. spending carelessly or lavishly

2. **emigrate**
    a. get rid of entirely
    b. remove guilt
    c. call forth
    d. sap vigor or strength
    e. leave one country for another

LESSON IX: EX-, EQUI-, EXTRA-

3. **eminent**
   a. prominent or distinguished
   b. gradual process of wear
   c. beyond what is reasonable
   d. spending carelessly or lavishly
   e. outside regular course of study

4. **enervate**
   a. call forth
   b. sap vigor or strength
   c. remove guilt
   d. leave one country for another
   e. cut out; remove

5. **equilateral**
   a. having sides of different lengths
   b. removing one side
   c. having all sides of the same length
   d. saving all pieces
   e. having different opinions

6. **equilibrium**
   a. equal share
   b. balance
   c. gradual incline
   d. angry state of mind
   e. shutting out of others

7. **equity**
   a. value of notes
   b. cost of bond shares
   c. equal distribution of shares
   d. fairness, justice
   e. quality of being partial

8. **equivalent**
   a. inequity
   b. equal in value, amount, etc.
   c. two dissimilar things
   d. unequal in value, cost, etc.
   e. lighting up

9. **eradicate**
   a. remove guilt
   b. leave one country for another
   c. get rid of entirely
   d. sap vigor or strength
   e. call forth

10. **erosion**
    a. remove guilt
    b. outside regular course of study
    c. prominent or distinguished
    d. gradual process of wear
    e. sap vigor or strength

11. **evoke**
    a. call forth
    b. get rid of entirely
    c. sap vigor or strength
    d. remove guilt
    e. cut out; remove

12. **excise**
    a. cut out; remove
    b. sap vigor or strength
    c. spending carelessly or lavishly
    d. outside regular course of study
    e. leave one country for another

13. **exclusive**
    a. shutting out all or most others
    b. spending carelessly or lavishly
    c. beyond what is reasonable
    d. prominent or distinguished
    e. gradual process of wear

14. **exhilarate**
    a. sap vigor or strength
    b. call forth
    c. remove guilt
    d. spend carelessly or lavishly
    e. make lively

15. **exonerate**
    a. call forth
    b. declare not guilty
    c. sap vigor or strength
    d. cut out; to remove
    e. spend carelessly or lavishly

LESSON IX: EX-, EQUI-, EXTRA-

16. **exorbitant**
    a. beyond what is reasonable
    b. gradual process of wear
    c. outside regular course of study
    d. prominent or distinguished
    e. spending lavishly

17. **extracurricular**
    a. outside regular course of study
    b. gradual process of wear
    c. beyond what is reasonable
    d. spending carelessly or lavishly
    e. prominent or distinguished

18. **extraneous**
    a. leave one country for another
    b. beyond what is reasonable
    c. gradual process of wear
    d. outside regular course of study
    e. unessential, peripheral

19. **extravagant**
    a. outside regular course of study
    b. spending carelessly or lavishly
    c. gradual process of wear
    d. dramatic
    e. prominent or distinguished

20. **extrovert**
    a. outside regular course of study
    b. outside the norm
    c. gradual process of wear
    d. leave one country for another
    e. outgoing person

Exercise D

Solve the crossword puzzle.

Across

4. To develop or present in further detail. 6. The process or result of gradually wearing away. 8. To bring or recall to the conscious mind. 10. To cut out surgically; to remove from a text or piece of music. 11. A state in which opposing forces or influences are balanced; a calm state of mind. 12. To remove or destroy completely. 13. Equal in value, amount, function, meaning, etc. 14. To officially absolve from blame. 15. To make very happy or animated. 16. Irrelevant or unrelated to the subject.

Down

1. Lacking restraint in spending money or using resources. 2. To leave one's own country to settle in another. 3. Equal-sided. 4. (Of an activity at school) pursued in addition to the normal curriculum. 5. (Of a price or amount) unreasonably high. 7. Excluding other things; restricted to the person, group, or area concerned; high-class. 9. To cause to feel drained of energy. 11. An outgoing person. 12. Respected and distinguished; notable. 15. Fairness and impartiality; the value of shares issued by a company.

Lesson X:
In-, Il-, Im-, Ir-

IN-, IL-, IM-, IR-
in, on, upon

illuminate, illustrate, imbibe, immigrate, imminent, impel, implicate, impression, impugn, incarcerate, incise, inclusive, indorse, induct, inscribe, insurgent, intend, invite, invocation, irradiate

Word Definitions

illuminate
v. to light up
"Large windows <u>illuminated</u> the upper floors, while the finished basement had recessed lighting."
illumination (n.)
illuminare to illuminate: *il-* (expressing intensity) + *luminare* to light up

illustrate
v. to provide with pictures; to show or demonstrate
"What examples <u>illustrate</u> the decline of the Roman Empire?"
illustration (n.), illustrative (adj.)
illustrare to make clear: *il-* on + *lustrare* to illuminate, to inspect

imbibe
v. to drink (especially alcohol); to take in (ideas or learning)
"Harrison reportedly died from <u>imbibing</u> ice water at his inauguration."
imbibere to drink in, to assimilate; *im-* in + *bibere* to drink

immigrate
v. to come to live permanently in a foreign county
"The Stapczynski's were not allowed to <u>immigrate</u> to America because U.S. law restricts the number of immigrants."
immigration (n.), immigrant (n.)
immigrare to immigrate: *im-* into + *migrare* to move

imminent	**adj.** about to happen; impending "Gathering gray clouds signaled a thunderstorm was imminent." *imminence (n.)* *imminere* to overhang, to impend: *im-* upon, toward + *minere* to project
impel	**v.** to force or to urge to do something "The quest for fame impelled Alexander to conquer the world." *impellere* to persuade, to urge on: *im-* toward + *pellere* to drive
implicate	**v.** to show to be involved in a crime or mishap; to incriminate "A faulty tile was implicated in the failure of the space shuttle." *implication (n.)* *implicare* to involve, to entangle: *im-* in + *plicare* to fold
impression	**n.** an idea, feeling, or opinion "Her intelligent and sympathetic manner made a good impression." *impress (v.)* *imprimere* to impress, to print: *im-* into + *premere* to press
impugn	**v.** to dispute or attack the truth, validity, or honesty of "The prosecutor impugned the defendant's character." *impugnare* to attack: *im-* into + *pugnare* to fight
incarcerate	**v.** to imprison or confine "Hardened convicts were incarcerated in Sing-Sing." *incarcerate (n.)* *incarcerare* imprison, confine: *in-* into + *carcer* prison, jail
incise	**v.** to make a cut or cuts in "The cook's cutting board was incised with knife marks." *incidere* to cut into: *in-* into + *caedere* to cut
inclusive	**adj.** including the limits specified; containing as part of whole "The numbers 0 to 9 comprise 10 digits inclusive." *includere* to imprison, to enclose: *in-* into + *claudere* to shut
indorse/endorse	**v.** to declare one's public approval of; to write on a document "Famous athletes are hired to promote and endorse athletic gear." *in-* in, on + *dorsum* back
induct	**v.** to admit formally to a post or organization "Caligula insisted that his horse be inducted as a Roman senator." *inducere* to lead in: *in-* into + *ducere* to lead
inscribe	**v.** to write or carve on a surface; to write a dedication to someone "The Rosetta Stone was inscribed in three different languages." *inscribere* to write on, to record: *in-* on + *scribere* to write
insurgent	**n.** a rebel or revolutionary "Spartacus was a slave insurgent who led a rebellion against Rome." *insurgence (n.)* *insurgere* to rise up against: *in-* (expressing intensity) + *surgere* to rise

intend	**v.** to have in mind; to plan "The actual results may differ from what you intend." *intendere* to intend, to direct: *in-* toward + *tendere* to stretch
invite	**v.** to ask in a friendly or formal way "Lack of an obviously strong defense may invite foreign invasion." *invitare* to invite (opposite of *vitare*, to avoid or shun)
invocation	**n.** a prayer calling on God; an appeal to authority "The priest began the service with an invocation." invocatory (adj.), invoke (v.) *invocare* to call upon, to pray for: *in-* upon + *vocare* to call
irradiate	**v.** to expose to radiation; to shine light upon "Irradiated food has a longer shelf life." *irradiare* to shine upon: *in-* upon + *radiare* to shine

EXERCISE A

Fill in the blanks in the sentences below with the correct form of a word in the scroll above.

1. The couple wanted to _____ all their friends to the wedding, but the size of the church limited their guest list.

2. A special celebration was planned to _____ the newest members of the club.

3. After much urging from the salesman, we felt _____ to purchase a new rather than a used car.

4. After he was _____ by the unions and the news media, the candidate's chances of winning the election were excellent.

5. For people living near the nuclear power plant, a fear of _____ was omnipresent.

6. From the _____ to the benediction, the children squirmed in the pew.

7. They _____ to finish the project quickly but faced unexpected delays.

8. We did not realize until later that we had been in _____ danger of attack by crocodiles while we were crossing the river.

9. The wooden desk was _____ with hack marks, left by decades of bored pupils playing with their penknives.

LESSON X: IN-, IL-, IM-, IR-

10. Adding a new porch lamp will _____ the front door and steps.

11. The last phase of the trial will determine the length of the murderer's _____.

12. His unkempt hair and mismatched clothes left a poor _____ on the interviewer.

13. New Year's Eve is a classic occasion to _____, especially champagne.

14. Everyone in line at the store was waiting for the author to _____ his signature on a copy of the bestselling book.

15. The witness could not testify without _____ herself in the crime.

16. The club was very _____; anyone interested in coin collecting was welcome.

17. At one time in our history, to _____ to America meant passing through Ellis Island.

18. In the novel, the main character _____ the will and maligns the other family members to gain a greater share of the inheritance.

19. Each year, there are separate awards for the text and _____ of notable new books.

20. Even after the main battle was won, various _____ continued to attack the soldiers.

EXERCISE B

Match the word with the letter of its definition.

1. **illuminate**
2. **illustrate**
3. **imbibe**
4. **immigrate**
5. **imminent**
6. **impel**
7. **implicate**
8. **impression**
9. **impugn**
10. **incarcerate**
11. **incise**
12. **inclusive**
13. **indorse/endorse**
14. **induct**
15. **inscribe**
16. **insurgent**
17. **intend**
18. **invite**
19. **invocation**
20. **irradiate**

a) idea, feeling, or opinion
b) provide with pictures
c) admit formally to a post or organization
d) show to be involved in a crime
e) ask in a friendly or formal way
f) dispute the truth, validity, or honesty of
g) declare one's public approval of
h) light up
i) rebel or revolutionary
j) imprison or confine
k) about to happen
l) drink
m) including the limits specified
n) have in mind; plan
o) expose to radiation
p) prayer calling on God
q) force or urge to do something
r) write on a surface
s) make a cut or cuts in
t) come to live permanently in a foreign county

LESSON X: IN-, IL-, IM-, IR-

EXERCISE C

Circle the letter of the definition which best fits the meaning of the bold-faced word.

1. **illuminate**
   a. resolve a problem
   b. provide with pictures
   c. discuss openly
   d. darken
   e. light up

2. **illustrate**
   a. write an inscription
   b. repeat
   c. provide with pictures
   d. write a story
   e. light up

3. **imbibe**
   a. swear
   b. drink
   c. catch a cold
   d. eat
   e. pray

4. **immigrate**
   a. come to live in a foreign county
   b. take a vacation
   c. leave a foreign country
   d. return to a country of origin
   e. visit a foreign country

5. **imminent**
   a. dangerous
   b. imprisoned
   c. about to happen
   d. leafy
   e. about to end

6. **impel**
   a. think for one's self
   b. force or urge to do something
   c. encourage someone
   d. commit to something
   e. imprison someone

7. **implicate**
   a. appoint a prosecutor
   b. defend a witness
   c. be imprisoned
   d. show to be involved in a crime
   e. commit a crime

8. **impression**
   a. idea, feeling, or opinion
   b. supposition based on prior knowledge
   c. premonition or foretelling
   d. dangerous or horrifying adventure
   e. past occurrence

9. **impugn**
   a. argue an insanity plea
   b. prove the truth about something
   c. rebel
   d. punish someone
   e. cast doubt on

10. **incarcerate**
    a. cut into or divide
    b. imprison or confine
    c. pierce with a weapon
    d. conduct a concert
    e. celebrate

11. **incise**
    a. examine
    b. make a cut or cuts in
    c. have a plan
    d. carve a sign
    e. make handicrafts

LESSON X: IN-, IL-, IM-, IR-

12. **inclusive**
    a. excluding certain characteristics
    b. exercising control over
    c. comprehensive, all encompassing
    d. involving specific cases
    e. having no limits

13. **indorse/endorse**
    a. move away
    b. declare officially over
    c. disapprove of
    d. declare one's approval of
    e. care for one's self

14. **induct**
    a. come together for a specific purpose
    b. drink to excess
    c. admit to a crime
    d. offer a prayer
    e. admit formally to a post or organization

15. **inscribe**
    a. dedicate to a cause
    b. ask in a friendly way
    c. write or carve on a surface
    d. force something
    e. light up

16. **insurgent**
    a. officer or gentleman
    b. enemy force
    c. incumbent
    d. rebel or revolutionary
    e. type of insurance

17. **intend**
    a. come together
    b. have in mind, plan
    c. create tension
    d. forget
    e. introduce someone

18. **invite**
    a. ask in a friendly or formal way
    b. plan a party
    c. write a message
    d. ask for money
    e. write an inscription

19. **invocation**
    a. wordy text
    b. invitation
    c. a prayer appealing to God
    d. refusal
    e. words of blessing

20. **irradiate**
    a. expose to cold
    b. expose to carbon dioxide
    c. expose to radiation
    d. expose to air
    e. protect from radioactivity

LESSON X: IN-, IL-, IM-, IR-

Exercise D

Solve the crossword puzzle:

Across
6. to show to be involved in a crime or mishap
8. to light up
9. to expose to radiation
10. including the limits specified
13. a prayer calling on God
15. to provide with pictures
16. to declare one's public approval of
17. a rebel or revolutionary

Down
1. to force or to urge to do something 2. to come to live permanently in a foreign county 3. to imprison or confine
4. to dispute or attack the truth, validity, or honesty of
5. an idea, feeling, or opinion 7. about to happen
8. to write or carve on a surface 11. to ask in a friendly or formal way 12. to make a cut or cuts in
13. to drink (especially alcohol)
14. to admit formally to a post or organization
17. to have in mind

Lesson XI:
Il-, Im-, In-, Ir-

IL-, IM-, IN-, IR-
not, against

illegible, illiterate, immaculate, immature, impeccable, implacable, impunity, inaccessible, incessant, inefficient, inflexible, ingratitude, inhospitable, inordinate, insoluble, insubordinate, irregular, irrelevant, irreverent, irrevocable

Word Definitions

illegible **adj.** not clear enough to be read
"'Cacography' is unreadable or illegible handwriting."
illegibility (n.)
il- not + *legere* to read

illiterate **adj.** unable to read or write
"Uniformly illiterate, pharaohs relied on scribes to read and write." *illiteracy (n.)*
il- not + *littera* letter, books

immaculate **adj.** perfectly clean, neat, or tidy; free from flaws or mistakes "Operating rooms must be kept immaculate to prevent infection." *immaculatus* without stain: *im-* not + *macula* spot, stain, blemish

immature **adj.** not fully developed; emotionally childish for one's age "A tadpole is the immature form of a frog."
immaturity (n.)
immaturus untimely, unripe: *im-* not + *maturus* timely, ripe

LESSON XI: IL-, IM-, IN-, IR-

impeccable   **adj.** in accordance with the highest standards; flawless
"Harvard and MIT degrees make for impeccable credentials."
impeccability (n.)
im- not + *peccabilis* sinful < *pecare* to sin

implacable   **adj.** unable to be appeased; relentless
"The families of Romeo and Juliet were implacable enemies."
implacability (n.)
im- not + *placare* to appease

impunity   **n.** exemption from punishment; freedom from harmful consequences of an action
"The 007 license allowed James Bond to kill with impunity."
impunis unpunished: *im-* not + *punire* to punish

inaccessible   **adj.** unable to be reached; difficult to understand or appreciate
"The 'red phone' is inaccessible to anyone but the president."
in- not + *accedere* to approach

incessant   **adj.** (especially of something unpleasant) continuing without pause or interruption
"A beehive is an incessant buzz of activity."
in- not + *cessare* to cease

inefficient   **adj.** unable to perform effectively or achieve maximum productivity; wasteful of time or resources
"A gasoline engine is less efficient than an electric one."
inefficiency (n.)
in- not + *efficere* to accomplish

inflexible   **adj.** unwilling or unable to change; stiff; rigid
"The Puritans were inflexible in their dress and church habits."
inflexibility (n.)
in- not + *flectere* to bend

ingratitude   **n.** a discreditable lack of thankfulness
"Failure to acknowledge a gift is a mark of ingratitude."
ingratus not thankful: *in-* not + *gratus* pleasing, thankful

inhospitable   **adj.** unwelcoming; harsh and difficult to live in
"The Sahara Desert is largely inhospitable to vegetation."
in- not + *hospes* host, guest

inordinate   **adj.** unusually large, excessive; past reasonable limits
"A heat wave placed inordinate demands on the electric power grid."
inordinatus: in- not + *ordinatus* to set in order, arrange

insoluble   **adj.** (of a substance) incapable of being dissolved; impossible to solve
"Until Newton, the nature of light appeared to be an insoluble problem."
insolubility (n.)
in- not + *solvere* to loosen, unfasten

LESSON XI: IL-, IM-, IN-, IR-

insubordinate **adj.** defiant of authority
"The soldier was <u>insubordinate</u>; he failed to carry out the colonel's orders."
insubordination (n.)
in- not + *subordinatus* lower in rank: *sub-* below + *ordinare* to set in order

irregular **adj.** contrary to or outside of a rule, authority, standard, or convention; not regular in shape, arrangement, or occurrence
"The Minutemen constituted an <u>irregular</u> fighting force."
irregularity (n.)
ir- not + *regula* rule, ruler, standard

irrelevant **adj.** not closely connected to (something); not mattering; unimportant
"Since all work was done indoors, the weather was <u>irrelevant</u>."
irrelevance (n.)
ir- not + *relevare* to raise up

irreverent **adj.** disrespectful
"The students' mocking skit was <u>irreverent</u> toward the faculty."
irreverence (n.)
ir- not + *revereri* to respect; to fear

irrevocable **adj.** unable to be recovered, annulled, or undone
"A contract, once signed, is usually <u>irrevocable</u>."
irrevocability (n.)
ir- not + *revocare* to recall, to regain, to revive: *re-* back + *vocare* to call

EXERCISE A

Fill in the blanks in the sentences below with the correct form of a word in the scroll above.

1. Although Reese declared the first take _____, director Steven Spielberg, a perfectionist, insisted on shooting the courtroom scene thirty times.

2. Paris Hilton spent such an _____ amount of time primping and preening in front of her vanity, Nikki hardly had time to prepare herself for the MTV Video Awards.

3. Her _____ comments amused her colleagues but upset her boss, who was very loyal to the company.

4. He was _____ in insisting his translation was the correct one.

5. Although she loves all the plants in her garden equally, Mrs. Wilson pays extra attention to
the _____ buds to make sure they blossom.

6. Doctors are required to sign so many documents each day, their signatures rapidly become _____ strings of loops and lines.

LESSON XI: IL-, IM-, IN-, IR-

7. John was fired for being _____ after he criticized his boss's plan to restructure the company.

8. June's belittling comments caused _____ damage to her relationship with Sasha.

9. Some college athletes can neglect their studies with _____ as long as they perform well on the field.

10. SUVs are extremely _____ compared to the compact hybrid cars made by Toyota and Honda.

11. The public refuses to embrace Barry Bonds despite his immense talent because of his perceived _____ for the natural gifts given to him.

12. Martha Stewart plans to keep her cell as _____ as she once kept her kitchen; even the warden will be required to remove his shoes before stepping inside.

13. Mars, a barren rock _____ to life, was once a matrix of rushing rivers and vast oceans capable of inhabitation by our purported ancestors, the protozoa.

14. A person's wealth should be _____ to his human rights.

15. When the tutor's student asked to switch his appointment from 11:30 to 11:00, the tutor replied that he could not honor the request because his hours were _____.

16. Because of construction in the kitchen, the appliances will be _____ for a week.

17. Creating stable and well-balanced economies in third-world countries is a momentous task, because in many nations most workers are _____ and therefore ill-equipped to handle jobs that require reading or writing.

18. The _____ call of the raven in Edgar Allen Poe's eponymous poem drives the narrator to madness.

19. We were granted a permit to build an _____ addition that was not in compliance with current zoning regulations.

20. Unlike salt or sugar, coal is _____ in water.

EXERCISE B

Match the word with the letter of its definition.

1. **illegible**
2. **illiterate**
3. **immaculate**
4. **immature**
5. **impeccable**
6. **implacable**
7. **impunity**
8. **inaccessible**
9. **incessant**
10. **inefficient**
11. **inflexible**
12. **ingratitude**
13. **inhospitable**
14. **inordinate**
15. **insoluble**
16. **insubordinate**
17. **irregular**
18. **irrelevant**
19. **irreverent**
20. **irrevocable**

a) not yet fully physically or emotionally grown
b) not easily bent, unalterable
c) exceeding reasonable limits
d) wasteful of time, energy, or materials
e) out of the ordinary
f) unwilling to obey authority
g) difficult or impossible to read
h) unable to be appeased or satisfied
i) flawless
j) disrespectful
k) incapable of being dissolved
l) unalterable; irreversible
m) continuing without interruption
n) unable to read
o) hostile or unfriendly; unfavorable to life
p) protection from punishment or harm
q) not topical; off subject
r) spotless; unblemished
s) lack of thankfulness
t) unable to be reached

EXERCISE C

Circle the letter of the definition that best fits the meaning of the bold-faced word.

1. **illegible**
   a. exceeding reasonable limits
   b. unable to read
   c. not included within a group
   d. difficult or impossible to read
   e. out of the usual

2. **illiterate**
   a. wasteful of time, energy, or materials
   b. unable to read
   c. continuing without interruption
   d. difficult or impossible to read
   e. disrespectful

3. **immaculate**
   a. perfectly pure, spotless
   b. out of the ordinary
   c. unable to read
   d. not to the point
   e. wasteful of time, energy, or materials

4. **immature**
   a. not to the point
   b. not yet full-grown
   c. lacking thankfulness
   d. exceeding reasonable limits
   e. perfect, incapable of error

5. **impeccable**
   a. lacking thankfulness
   b. free of error
   c. out of the ordinary
   d. lacking maturity
   e. disrespectful

6. **implacable**
   a. not to the point
   b. perfect, incapable of error
   c. unable to be appeased or satisfied
   d. difficult or impossible to read
   e. disrespectful

7. **impunity**
   a. lack of thankfulness
   b. arrogance, a sense of entitlement
   c. total solitude
   d. difficulty in understanding language
   e. protection from punishment or harm

8. **inaccessible**
   a. unable to attend
   b. able to reason
   c. unable to be satisfied
   d. unable to be reached
   e. able to be satisfied

9. **incessant**
   a. continuing without interruption
   b. not easily bent, unalterable
   c. lacking a rational reason
   d. unalterable, irreversible
   e. unwilling to obey authority

10. **inefficient**
    a. unwilling to obey authority
    b. unable to be satisfied
    c. lacks a rational reason
    d. unalterable, irreversible
    e. wasteful of time, energy, or materials

LESSON XI: IL-, IM-, IN-, IR-

11. **inflexible**
    a. rigid
    b. exceeding reasonable limits
    c. unable to read
    d. hostile or unfriendly; unfavorable to life
    e. not easily bent, unalterable

12. **ingratitude**
    a. dedication ceremony
    b. lack of thankfulness
    c. tip left for someone who has provided a service
    d. cruelty
    e. protection from punishment or harm

13. **inhospitable**
    a. hostile or unfriendly; unfavorable to life
    b. lacking thankfulness
    c. exceeding reasonable limits
    d. unwilling to obey authority
    e. perfectly pure, spotless

14. **inordinate**
    a. unwilling to obey authority
    b. lacking maturity
    c. exceeding reasonable limits
    d. not able to be appeased or satisfied
    e. unable to be satisfied

15. **insoluble**
    a. easy to solve
    b. incapable of being dissolved
    c. protected by water
    d. capable of being dissolved
    e. probable cause

16. **insubordinate**
    a. protection from punishment or harm
    b. defiant of authority
    c. lacks a rational reason
    d. continuing without interruption
    e. not easily bent, unalterable

17. **irregular**
    a. hostile or unfriendly, unfavorable to life
    b. out of the ordinary
    c. unable to read
    d. continuing without interruption
    e. lacking maturity

18. **irrelevant**
    a. protection from punishment or harm
    b. hostile or unfriendly; unfavorable to life
    c. perfectly pure, spotless
    d. beside the point
    e. impossible to solve or explain

19. **irreverent**
    a. hostile or unfriendly; unfavorable to life
    b. disrespectful
    c. perfectly pure, spotless
    d. impossible to solve or explain
    e. protection from punishment or harm

20. **irrevocable**
    a. protection from punishment or harm
    b. stiff, hard to bend
    c. lacks a rational reason
    d. unalterable, irreversible
    e. impossible to solve or explain

LESSON XI: IL-, IM-, IN-, IR-

Exercise D

Solve the crossword puzzle.

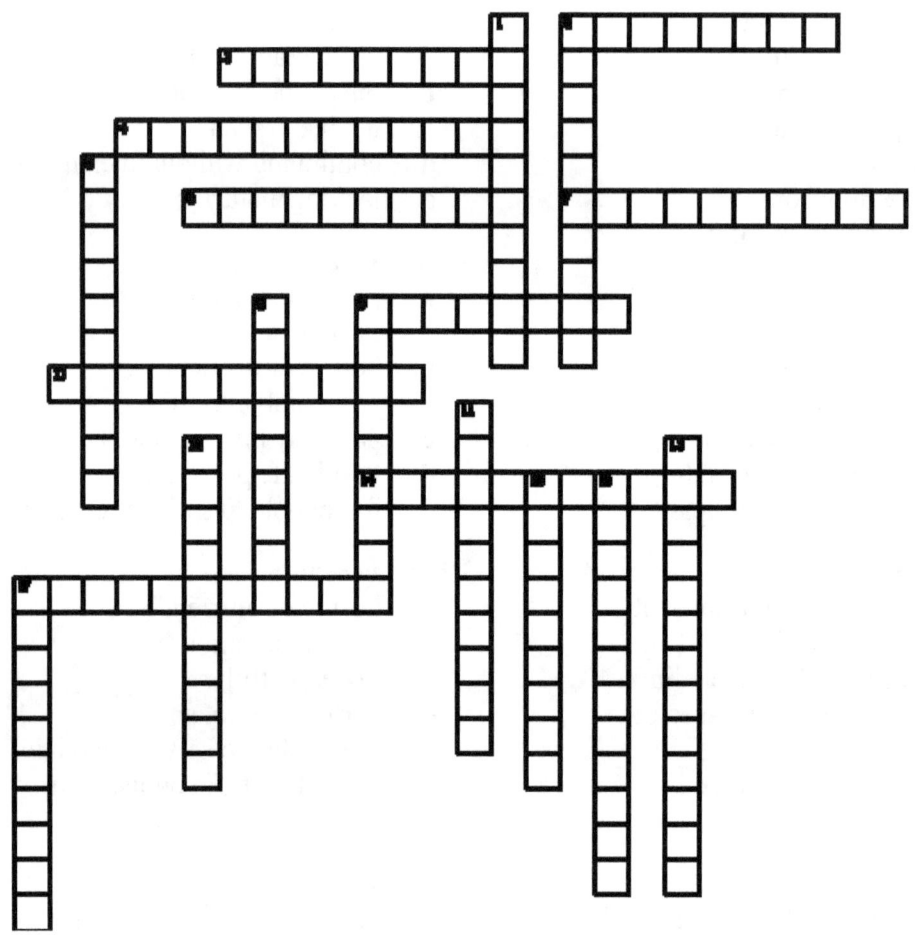

Across
2. Not fully developed. 3. Contrary to a rule, standard, or convention; not regular in shape, arrangement, or occurrence. 4. Unable to be reached; difficult to understand or appreciate. 6. In accordance with the highest standards. 7. Perfectly clean, neat, or tidy; free from flaws or mistakes. 9. Exemption from punishment or freedom from harmful consequences of an action. 10. Not able to be recovered, annulled, or undone. 14. Not achieving maximum productivity; failing to make the best use of time or resources. 17. A discreditable lack of thankfulness.

Down
1. Not closely connected to or appropriate for the matter at hand. 2. Unusually large, excessive; past reasonable limits. 5. Disrespectful. 8. (Especially of something unpleasant) continuing without pause or interruption. 9. Not clear enough to be read. 11. Unwilling to change; not able to be changed or adapted. 12. Unable to read or write. 13. Defiant of authority. 15. (Of a substance) incapable of being dissolved; impossible to solve. 16. Harsh and difficult to live in; unwelcoming to life. 17. Unable to be appeased; unable to be stopped; unimpeachable.

LESSON XI:IL-, IM-, IN-, IR-

Test 2

1. "A slight down on her upper lip, about the corners, began to spread and darken like a trail of smoke; her temples grew shiny; <u>decadence</u> was beginning!"

   An Old Maid by Honore de Balzac

   (a) moral or physical decline (b) lower quality (c) devotion to a task
   (d) diminishing importance (e) drunken and disorderly

2. "Under foot the leaves were dry, and the foliage of some holly bushes which grew among the <u>deciduous</u> trees was dense enough to keep off draughts."

   Tess of the d'Urbervilles by Thomas Hardy

   (a) permanent condition (b) perennial (c) shedding annually
   (d) creative (e) coniferous

3. "Every living creature there held life as of no account, and was <u>demented</u> with a passionate readiness to sacrifice it."

   A Tale Of Two Cities by Charles Dickens

   (a) eager (b) insane (c) comely (d) poor (e) fallen

4. "I am the lineal <u>descendant</u> of that infant -- I am the rightful Duke of Bridgewater; and here am I, forlorn, torn from my high estate, hunted of men, despised by the cold world, ragged, worn, heart-broken, and degraded to the companionship of felons on a raft."

   Adventures of Huckleberry Finn by Mark Twain

   (a) neighbor (b) parent (c) sibling (d) offspring (e) ancestor

5. " I sat about in the darkness of the scullery, in a state of <u>despondent</u> wretchedness."

   The War of the Worlds by H.G. Wells

   (a) determined (b) dejected (c) supported (d) complete
   (e) contemptible

93

6. "Fogg, in order not to deviate from his course, furled his sails and increased the force of the steam; but the vessel's speed slackened, owing to the state of the sea, the long waves of which broke against the stern."
Around The World in Eighty Days by Jules Verne

    (a) rely   (b) abandon   (c) knock down
    (d) diminish in importance   (e) swerve

7. "He was too diffident to do justice to himself; but when his natural shyness was overcome, his behaviour gave every indication of an open, affectionate heart."
Sense and Sensibility by Jane Austen

    (a) timid   (b) neglected (c) discontented   (d) ruined
    (e) rebel

8. "Then listen, not to dulcet harmony, But to a discord wrung by mad despair Out of this bosom's depths of bitterness, To ease my heart and plant a sting in thine."
Don Quixote by Miguel Cervantes

    (a) unhappiness   (b) lack of courage   (c) lack of agreement or harmony
    (d) lack of reputation (e) lack of confidence

9. "But the lovely aromas in that enchanted air did at last seem to dispel, for a moment, the cankerous thing in his soul."
Moby Dick by Herman Melville

    (a) break into small pieces   (b) scatter or make disappear
    (c) express disagreement   (d) make feelings   (e) magnify

10. "Upon my word," Luzhin cried wrathfully and irritably, crimson with confusion, "to distort my words in this way!"
Crime And Punishment by Fyodor Dostoyevsky

    (a) exaggerate (b) blend together (c) mimic (d) criticize (e) misrepresent

11. "And so it was that I, the modern, often entered into my dreaming, and in the consequent strange dual personality was both actor and spectator."
Before Adam by Jack London

    (a) separate (b) double   (c) bizarre   (d) deceitful (e) ancient

12. "She suddenly felt ashamed of her duplicity, but even more she dreaded how he might meet her."

Anna Karenina by Leo Tolstoy

(a) distrust (b) recognition (c) satisfaction (d) deception (e) appearance

13. "It is on record that three times nearly all the inhabitants have been obliged to emigrate to the south."

The Voyage of the Beagle by Charles Darwin

(a) leave permanently (b) return (c) homestead (d) develop (e) travel

14. "What is the nature of the luxury which enervates and destroys nations?"

Walden by Henry David Thoreau

(a) removes (b) overcomes (c) becomes nervous (d) cuts out (e) weakens

15. "The genius of the people will ill brook the inquisitive and peremptory spirit of excise laws."

Federalist Papers by Alexander Hamilton

(a) arbitrary (b) popular (c) blame (d) tax (e) unfair

16. "Thus by a judicious exercise of tact and asperity we re-established the atmospheric equilibrium of the room long before I left them a little before midnight, now tenderly reconciled, to walk down to the harbour and hail the Tremolino by the usual soft whistle from the edge of the quay."

The Mirror of the Sea by Joseph Conrad

(a) fairness (b) balance (c) currents (d) temperature (e) safety

17. "The reason thereof is that he carrieth too many extraneous things on his shoulders."

Thus Spake Zarathustra by Friedrich Nietzsche

(a) heavy (b) uncomfortable (c) irrelevant (d) incoming (e) confident

18. "My state of mind regarding the pilfering from which I had been so unexpectedly exonerated, did not impel me to frank disclosure; but I hope it had some dregs of good at the bottom of it."
Great Expectations by Charles Dickens

    (a) expose   (b) prevent   (c) obscure   (d) confine   (e) motivate

19. "Fearing in his heart lest this might prove but too true, the captain a little desisted, but still commanded the insurgents instantly to return to their duty."
Moby Dick by Herman Melville

    (a) immigrants (b) rebels   (c) officers   (d) incumbents   (e) soldiers

20. "And the invocation was uttered in such a tone as to indicate a rooted antipathy to anything so commonplace, even if she had not added that sequins gave her the sick."
Of Human Bondage by W. Somerset Maugham

    (a) soliloquy (b) invention (c) appeal   (d) offering   (e) dedication

21. "The old Squire was an implacable man: he made resolutions in violent anger, and he was not to be moved from them after his anger had subsided-- as fiery volcanic matters cool and harden into rock."
Silas Marner by George Eliot

    (a) restless   (b) relentless (c) unreadable (d) immature (e) extraordinary

22. "There was an incessant flow of people to and from Tampa Town and the place, which resembled a procession, or rather, in fact, a pilgrimage."
From the Earth to the Moon by Jules Verne

    (a) continuous   (b) unalterable   (c) irreversible
    (d) wasteful   (e) unruly

23. "There was no solution, but that universal solution which life gives to all questions, even the most complex and insoluble."
Anna Karenina by Leo Tolstoy

    (a) probable   (b) hostile   (c) impossible to explain
    (d) continuing without interruptions   (e) unfavorable

24. "'It may be so,' said the young clergyman, indifferently, as waiving a discussion that he considered <u>irrelevant</u> or unseasonable."

The Scarlet Letter by Nathaniel Hawthorne

    (a) disrespectful (b) obedient (c) ordinary   (d) extraneous (e) irrational

25. "This was greeted with an <u>irreverent</u> laugh, and the youth blushed deeply, and tried to look as if he had meant to insinuate what knowing people called a 'double entendre.'"

The Age of Innocence by Edith Wharton

    (a) harmless   (b) disrespectful   (c) extraneous (d) hurtful   (e) riotous

Lesson XII:
Inter-, Intra-

INTER-
among, between

INTRA-
within

intercede, interest, interjection, interlude, intermediary, intermission, intermittent, international, internecine, interpolate, interpret, interregnum, intersect, intervene, interstice, intramural, intravenous, introduce, introspection, introvert

Word Definitions

intercede
v. to act as a mediator in a dispute
"The U.S. interceded in the dispute between the Palestinians and Israelis."
interceder (n.)
intercedere to intervene: *inter-* between + *cedere* to go, to step aside

interest
v. to excite the curiosity or attention of (someone)
n. a desire to know more about something or someone; an additional sum paid for the use of loaned money
"Non-members have no interest in the club's proceedings."
interesting (adj.)
interesse to be in the midst of; to be different: *inter-* between + *esse* to be

interjection
n. a remark inserted when someone else is speaking; an exclamation
"'Ach!' is an interjection in both Scottish and German."
interject (v.)
interjacere to interpose or insert: *inter-* between + *jacere* to throw

interlude
n. a dissimilar event or period between two others; an intermission
"The Great Depression occurred during the interlude between world wars."
interludium interlude, episode: *inter-* between + *ludus* play

LESSON XII: INTER-, INTRA-

intermediary
n. a mediator; a go-between
adj. existing or occurring between
"Teachers should show the <u>intermediary</u> steps in solving math problems."
intermedius intermediate: *inter-* between + *medius* middle

intermission
n. a pause or break
"The break in the middle of a concert is called the <u>intermission</u>."
intermittere interrupt: *inter-* between + *mittere* to release, to dismiss

intermittent
adj. occurring at intervals; not continuous or steady
"A telephone has an <u>intermittent</u> rather than a constant ring."
intermittere interrupt: *inter-* between + *mittere* to release, to dismiss

international
adj. existing or occurring between nations
"<u>International</u> agreements involve two or more countries." *inter-* between + *natio* nation < *nat-, nasci* to be born

internecine
adj. a mutually destructive conflict; a struggle within a nation or group "Greek city-states were given to <u>internecine</u> warfare."
inter- among + *necare* to kill

interpolate
v. to interject; to insert new (often misleading) material into another's work "While editing the manuscript, he <u>interpolated</u> his own remarks."
interpolare to refurbish; to falsify: *inter-* between + *polare* to polish, to clean (variant of *polire*)

interpret
v. to explain the meaning of (words, actions, etc.); to perform in a way that conveys one's understanding of the creator's ideas
"A good translator <u>interprets</u> a poem as a whole, not word by word."
interpretation (n.)
interpretare to explain, to translate < *interpretis* translator, interpreter

interregnum
n. a period when normal government is suspended, especially between successive reigns or regimes
"Between Egypt's Old and New Kingdoms was an <u>interregnum</u>."
inter- between + *regnum* reign

intersect
v. to divide across or through; to cross (of roads, etc.); to meet at a point "The road near my house <u>intersects</u> a state highway."
intersection (n.)
intersecare to cut apart, to divide: *inter-* between + *secare* to cut

interstice
n. a small intervening space, crack, or fissure
"The message was hidden in an <u>interstice</u> between the inner and outer walls."
intersistere to stand between: *inter-* between + *sistere* to cause to stand up

intervene
v. to come between; to occur as an unplanned circumstance "The policeman <u>intervened</u> to end the fistfight." *intervention (n.)*
intervenire to come between: *inter-* between + *venire* to come

LESSON XII: INTER-, INTRA-

intramural adj. situated or done within a building, a school, or a community "Intramural sports take place within the college."
intra- between + *murus* wall

intravenous adj. within or into a vein or veins
"Medicines administered by needle or syringe are intravenous."
intra- within + *vena* vein

introduce v. to bring into use or operation for the first time; to present someone by name to another; to insert or bring into something
"He introduced his new girlfriend to his parents."
introduction (n.)
introducere to bring inside: *intro-* to the inside + *ducere* to lead

introspection n. the examination of one's own thoughts or feelings
"Buddha was given to long periods of introspection and meditation."
introspective (adj.)
intro- within + *spectare* to look

introvert n. a shy, reticent person (opposite of extrovert)
"An introvert, he greatly preferred an evening of reading to a party."
introversion (n.), introverted (adj.)
intro- to the inside + *vertere* to turn

EXERCISE A

Fill in the blanks in the sentences below with the correct form of a word in the scroll above.

1. The Jackson Five _____ the world to the young Michael Jackson, who later became the "King of Pop."

2. Eastern philosophy preaches searching not for what is valuable in the world, but searching for what is valuable in oneself through _____.

3. Arthur Miller's play *The Crucible,* based on the Salem witch trials, is often _____ as a metaphor for McCarthyism in the 1950's.

4. Stephen exclaimed "Holy cow!" when he saw the shooting star. This _____ failed to wake his brother, however.

5. New York City is easier to navigate than Boston, because New York streets _____ at right angles, while roads in Boston cross at arbitrary angles.

LESSON XII: INTER-, INTRA-

6. The falsely accused murder suspect prayed for someone with evidence absolving him of blame to _____ on his behalf.

7. Those athletes who are unable to make the varsity or junior varsity teams may participate in _____ sports.

8. During the intermission, the Boston Pops rested a brief _____ before returning to entertain the audience.

9. We watched the final inning of the World Series game with great _____.

10. The contractors blew insulation into the _____ between wall studs.

11. Some countries have an _____ period after one government dissolves and before a new one takes power.

12. He acted as an _____ during the periods when Joanne and Erika weren't speaking to each other.

13. The pain from the cavity was _____; at some points it was unnoticeable, at others it was unbearable.

14. _____ drugs affect the patient more rapidly than those taken orally because they enter the bloodstream directly.

15. Although he exudes confidence and charm on camera, Toby McGuire describes himself as an _____.

16. Leo _____ some verse from Shakespeare with his personal sentiments for Caitlin and won her heart with the passionate message.

17. _____ struggles within the tribes have led to countless casualties.

18. It is inappropriate for small children to _____ in adult affairs.

19. Steve went to the restroom a few minutes before the _____ to avoid the endless lines that form in the interlude between acts.

20. Although the media have focused on the American government's war on _____ terrorism, it is important to keep in mind that there are many dangerous terrorist groups within the U.S.

LESSON XII: INTER-, INTRA-

EXERCISE B

Match the word with the letter of its definition.

1. intercede
2. interest
3. interjection
4. interlude
5. intermediary
6. intermission
7. intermittent
8. international
9. internecine
10. interpolate
11. interpret
12. interregnum
13. intersect
14. intervene
15. interstice
16. intramural
17. intravenous
18. introduce
19. introspection
20. introvert

a) a period between two events
b) alter a text or composition
c) meet at a point; divide by crossing
d) exclamation
e) person who acts as a go-between
f) come between (to prevent or alter)
g) mutually destructive
h) act as a mediator
i) occurring at intervals
j) explain
k) pause or break in a performance
l) between nations
m) self-examination
n) within the walls of a school
o) desire to know about something
p) in the veins
q) small intervening space
r) acquaint (someone) with
s) suspension of government
t) person who does not easily share thoughts or feelings

EXERCISE C

Circle the letter of the definition that best fits the meaning of the bold-faced word.

1. **intercede**
   a. go between places
   b. place under
   c. act as a mediator
   d. fight
   e. disagree

2. **interest**
   a. desire to know about someone or something
   b. accounting for something
   c. not caring about anything
   d. giving away money
   e. slipping downhill

LESSON XII: INTER-, INTRA-

3. **interjection**
   a. explanation
   b. statement
   c. pause in conversation
   d. lengthy conversation
   e. exclamation

4. **interlude**
   a. politics between nations
   b. repetition in an aria
   c. explanation for time lost
   d. time between events
   e. imitation of something real

5. **intermediary**
   a. person who acts as a go-between
   b. merchant
   c. gas station attendant
   d. person who creates a disturbance
   e. medic in training

6. **intermission**
   a. competition
   b. break
   c. affair
   d. delay
   e. exclamation

7. **intermittent**
   a. occurring at intervals
   b. continuous motion
   c. sending a letter
   d. writing en route
   e. wiping a windshield

8. **international**
   a. between nations
   b. large in scope
   c. between states
   d. transcontinental
   e. south of the Equator

9. **internecine**
   a. constructive to all
   b. harmful to no one
   c. destructive on both sides
   d. fruitful
   e. joyful at times

10. **interpolate**
    a. meet at a point
    b. join at a seam
    c. sort by like qualities
    d. poll a population
    e. insert in a text or composition

11. **interpret**
    a. alter
    b. explain
    c. put in front
    d. come into view
    e. make a difference

12. **interregnum**
    a. rule to live by
    b. in between campaigns
    c. government regulation
    d. kingly lifestyle
    e. suspension of government

13. **intersect**
    a. have a conference
    b. meet at a point
    c. join together
    d. go around
    e. hurry away

14. **intervene**
    a. come into contact with
    b. surprise someone
    c. come between
    d. shrink back
    e. alter a text

15. **interstice**
    a. closet
    b. small space or crevice
    c. landscaped yard
    d. very large space
    e. residential building

16. **intramural**
    a. relating to sex
    b. pertaining to countries
    c. affecting those around
    d. pertaining to a school
    e. lifting heavy objects

LESSON XII: INTER-, INTRA-

Exercise D

Solve the crossword puzzle.

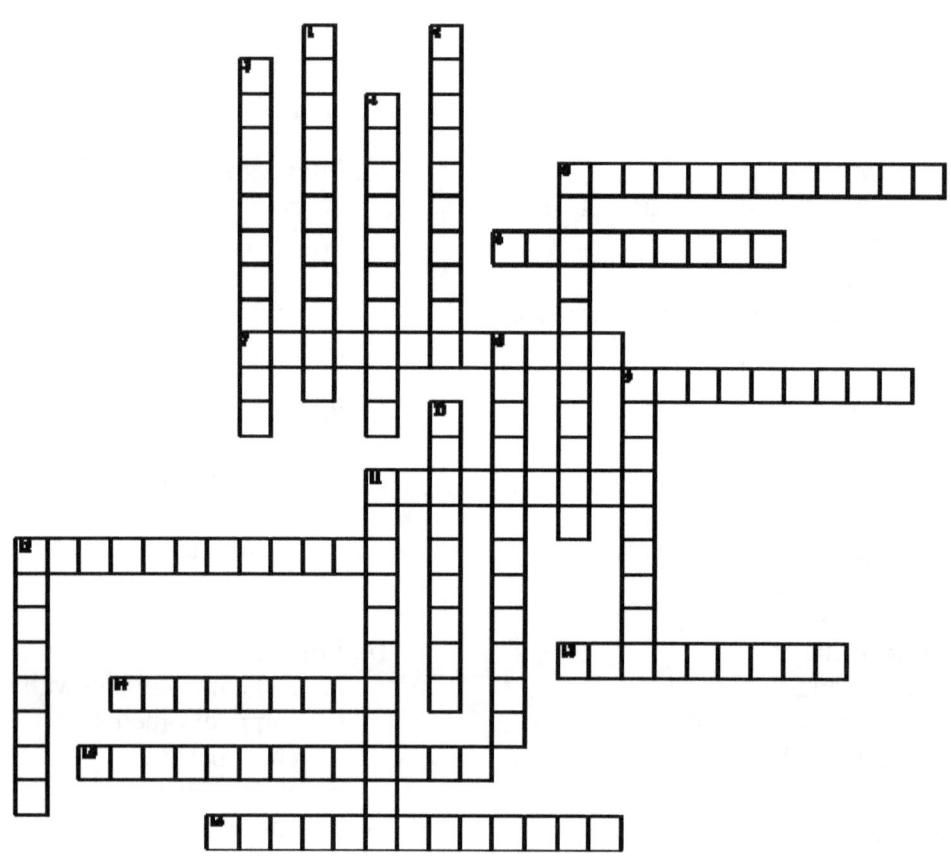

Across
5. A sudden, short utterance. 6. A shy, reticent person (opposite of extrovert). 7. A mediator; a go-between. 9. To bring into use or operation for the first time; to present someone by name to another; to insert or bring into something. 11. An intervening period of time; something occurring or done during an interval. 12. Occurring at irregular intervals, not continuous or steady. 13. To come between; to occur as an unplanned circumstance. 14. To act as a mediator in a dispute. 15. Existing or occurring between nations. 16. The examination of one's own thoughts or feelings.

Down
1. To insert (words) in a book, especially to give the false impression as to its date; to interject a remark in a conversation. 2. A small intervening space, crack, or fissure. 3. Destructive to both sides in a conflict; struggle within a nation or group. 4. Situated or done within a building, a single educational institution, or a community. 5. A period when normal government is suspended, especially between successive reigns or regimes. 8. A pause or break. 9. To divide something by passing or the fact of lying across it. 10. To explain the meaning of (words, actions, etc.); to perform in a way that conveys one's understanding of the creator's ideas. 11. Within or into a vein or veins. 12. To excite the curiosity or attention of.

Lesson XIII:
Magnus-, Mal-, Multi-

MAGNUS-	*MAL-*	*MULTI-*
big	bad	many

magnanimous, magnate, magnificent, magnitude, major, majority, maladjusted, malady, malaise, malediction, male/actor, malevolent, malicious, malign, malignant, malnutrition, malodorous, malpractice, multifarious, multilateral, multitude

Word Definitions

magnanimous **adj.** generous; kindhearted or forgiving
"Grant was magnanimous in allowing the rebels to keep their horses."
magnanimus generous, bold: *magnus* great + *animus* soul

magnate **n.** a wealthy and influential business person
"Andrew Carnegie was a 19th century steel magnate."
magnas great man < *magnus* great

magnificent **adj.** very beautiful, elaborate, or impressive
"The Great Pyramid is a magnificent tribute to King Khufu."
magnificare to prize, to praise: *magnus* great + *facere* to make

magnitude **n.** size, extent, or importance
"Matt realized the magnitude of the problem after he failed the test."
magnitudo size, bulk, greatness < *magnus* great

major **adj.** important, serious, or significant; great or large (in size)
n. a military or police rank; a student's principal course of study
"The constellation Ursa Major dwarfs Ursa Minor."
ma}or < *magnus* great

majority	**n.** more than half "A simple majority approved the measure, but the president vetoed it." *majoritas* greater size or rank < *major* < *magnus* great
maladjusted	**adj.** failing to cope with or fit into a normal social environment "Because of frequent moves, Army brats are often maladjusted." *mal-* bad + *ad-* to + *juxta* close by, near
malady	**n.** a disease, disorder, or ailment "A hypochondriac constantly complains of new ills and maladies." *malade* sick: *malus* ill, bad + *habere* to have or keep
malaise	**n.** a general feeling of discomfort or poor health; uneasiness "Depressed and slightly ill, the man was overcome by malaise." *mal-* bad + *aise* ease
malediction	**n.** speaking evil of or to another person; a curse "'Go to hell!' and 'Damn you!' exemplify curses or maledictions." *maledictive (adj.)* *maledicere* to speak evil of: *mal-* bad + *dicere to* say or speak
malefactor	**n.** a person who commits a crime or some other wrong "Thieves and murderers are two types of malefactors." *malefacere* to do wrong: *mal-* bad, evil + *facere* to do or make
malevolent	**adj.** wishing evil to others "After he found out Cheri had started the nasty rumors, James knew she was malevolent." *malevolence (n.)* *malevolentis* spiteful, malicious: *mal-* bad + *volentis* wish
malicious	**adj.** intending or intended to do harm "Sticking pins in a voodoo doll shows malicious intent." *malice (n.)* *malignus* tending to evil < *malus* bad
malign	**v.** to speak ill of, slander, or defame **adj.** evil in nature or effect "He maligned her when he testified that she was a habitual liar." *malignus* tending to evil < *malus* bad
malignant	**adj.** evil, malevolent; (of a tumor) harmful, growing out of control (opposite of benign) "Christians consider all malignant influences to be the work of the devil." *malignus* tending to evil < *malus* bad
malnutrition	**n.** a lack of proper nourishment caused by not having enough to eat or not eating the right things "Many children in poor nations die of malnutrition every year." *malnutritious (adj.)* *malus* bad + *nutrire* to suckle

LESSON XIII: MAGNUS-, MAL-, MULTI-

malodorous   **adj.** smelling very unpleasant
"Skunk cabbage is very malodorous when stepped on."
mal- bad + *odor* smell

malpractice   **n.** an improper, illegal, or negligent professional treatment
"Leaving gauze in a patient after surgery constitutes malpractice."
mal- bad + *practica* practice

multifarious   **adj.** having great variety and diversity
"The singer/dancer/songwriter had multifarious talents."
multifarius many-fold: *multi-* many + *feri* to be made

multilateral   **adj.** agreed upon or done by three or more political parties or nations
"The Group of Seven meetings involve multilateral talks."
multi- many + *latus* side

multitude   **n.** a large number of people or things; the mass of ordinary people
"A multitude of locusts blackened the sky, then alit in the cornfields."
multitudo great number, crowd or mob < *multus* many

EXERCISE A

Fill in the blanks in the sentences below with the correct form of a word in the scroll above.

1. The view outside Rachel's apartment window, of the setting sun casting a purple luminescence on the snow-encrusted mountains, was _____.

2. She _____ the dead mayor in an article, adding to the grief and humiliation of his family.

3. Upon selling Jordan's Furniture, the owners, Barry and Gordon, gave a _____ gift to their longest serving and most dedicated workers.

4. After decades of holding _____ jobs, she can do almost anything.

5. Until the doctors diagnosed the specific _____, they were only able to alleviate the patient's symptoms.

6. Harold did not know whether to declare physics or chemistry as his _____ in college.

7. A _____ with a string of convictions for assault, burglary and rape, Gerald was finally imprisoned for life.

8. He was clearly a _____ person, always hoping that others would be thwarted or humiliated.

LESSON XIII: MAGNUS-, MAL-, MULTI-

9. The _____ agreement among the western European nations will promote trade.

10. The ferocity of the tropical storm caught the deep sea fishing vessel by surprise; the crew was not expecting a tempest of such _____ .

11. The _____ thief stole the family's Christmas presents right before the holiday.

12. The witch cursed and heaped _____ on her innocent victims.

13. People who graduate from public high schools may seem _____ to college initially, compared with those who graduate from private ones.

14. *The Apprentice* is a hit show hosted by real estate mogul and business _____ Donald Trump.

15. In a democratic nation, a _____ vote usually determines who will be elected.

16. To prevent _____ during the famine, the Red Cross gave vitamins to as many people as possible.

17. Fortunately, a biopsy showed the tumor was benign, not_____ .

18. After scoring the winning goal in the World Cup, David Beckham smiled at the _____ of ecstatic fans before collapsing from exhaustion.

19. The garbage collectors soon got used to their _____ task.

20. When _____ insurance becomes too expensive, it drives doctors out of work.

EXERCISE B

Match the word with the letter of its definition.

1. magnanimous
2. magnate
3. magnificent
4. magnitude
5. major
6. majority
7. maladjusted
8. malady
9. malediction
10. malefactor
11. malevolent
12. malicious
13. malign
14. malignant
15. malnutrition
16. malodorous
17. malpractice
18. multifarious
19. multilateral
20. multitude

a) a great number
b) a curse
c) of great size or importance
d) to slander or defame
e) having great variety and diversity
f) harmful; growing out of control
g) wishing evil to others
h) lack of proper nourishment
i) agreed upon by more than three parties
j) negligent professional treatment
k) generous
l) more than half
m) not well adjusted socially
n) important, powerful business person
o) disease; disorder
p) spectacular, exceptional
q) person who commits a crime
r) smelling very unpleasant
s) scope, importance
t) intending to do harm

LESSON XIII: MAGNUS-, MAL-, MULTI-

EXERCISE C

Circle the letter of the definition that best fits the meaning of the bold-faced word.

1. **magnanimous**
   a. enormous
   b. egotistical
   c. generous
   d. insane
   e. kind

2. **magnate**
   a. strong attraction
   b. complex demand
   c. difficult decision
   d. powerful person
   e. public movement

3. **magnificent**
   a. small and insignificant
   b. spectacular, exceptional
   c. multicolored
   d. poor quality
   e. noble, prize-worthy

4. **magnitude**
   a. scope, importance
   b. bad attitude
   c. large ego
   d. geographical feature
   e. strong magnet

5. **major**
   a. of great importance or stature
   b. unimportant, insignificant
   c. incorrect or irrelevant
   d. serious, not funny
   e. trivial

6. **majority**
   a. most evidence
   b. smallest number
   c. least beautiful
   d. best outcome
   e. more than half

7. **maladjusted**
   a. well adjusted
   b. carefully completed
   c. does not fit in
   d. calmness
   e. difficult to finish

8. **malady**
   a. lady's purse
   b. game or type of entertainment
   c. corn or bulb
   d. ailment
   e. prize or award

9. **malediction**
   a. calling to someone
   b. curse
   c. writing bad things
   d. hearing evil
   e. seeing evil

10. **malefactor**
    a. person who saves money
    b. tractor driver
    c. soothing voice
    d. person who commits a crime
    e. wrongdoing

11. **malevolent**
    a. wishing evil to others
    b. doing wrong
    c. wishing goodwill to others
    d. coming together
    e. completing homework

12. **malicious**
    a. speaking evil
    b. tending to invade
    c. intending to do harm
    d. desiring evil
    e. abhorrent

LESSON XIII: MAGNUS-, MAL-, MULTI-

13. malign
   a. do physical harm
   b. desire help
   c. come between
   d. intend to do a crime
   e. defame

14. malignant
   a. characterized by good will
   b. attracting birds
   c. evil, harmful
   d. acting as a messenger
   e. relating to nobility

15. malnutrition
   a. lack of proper nutrition
   b. desire to overeat
   c. lack of water or liquid refreshment
   d. state of plenty
   e. hospital food

16. malodorous
   a. smelling fresh and sweet
   b. looking bad
   c. sounding loud
   d. smelling unpleasant
   e. looking wonderful

17. malpractice
   a. adequate care
   b. commitment issues
   c. practicing a musical instrument
   d. medical emergency
   e. negligent professional treatment

18. multifarious
   a. having many different elements
   b. untrustworthy, duplicitous
   c. full of surprises
   d. having many opinions
   e. strange; mysterious

19. multilateral
   a. having only one side
   b. painfully stubborn
   c. extremely lonely
   d. agreed upon by three or more parties
   e. ease of recognition

20. multitude
   a. mountain range
   b. incomplete set
   c. great number; collection
   d. confusing statement
   e. group of ideas

LESSON XIII: MAGNUS-, MAL-, MULTI-

Exercise D

Solve the crossword puzzle.

Across
2. Important, serious, or significant. 3. Smelling very unpleasantly. 5. A disease, disorder, or ailment. 6. Characterized by malice; intending or intended to do harm. 8. Very beautiful, elaborate, or impressive. 9. More than half. 12. Wishing evil to others. 13. Speaking evil of or to another person, a curse. 14. Having great variety and diversity. 15. Failing to cope with the demands of a normal social environment. 16. A person who commits a crime or some other wrong.

Down
1. A lack of proper nourishment, caused by not having enough to eat or not eating enough of the right things. 2. An improper, illegal, or negligent professional treatment. 4. To speak ill of, slander, or defame. 5. A general feeling of discomfort. 6. Agreed upon or participated in by three or more parties. 7. Size, extent, or importance. 8. Evil, malevolent; (of a tumor) tending to invade normal tissue or to recur after removal. 10. A large number of people or things; the mass of ordinary people. 11. A wealthy and influential business person. 14. Generous, kindhearted or forgiving.

Lesson XIV:
Ob-, Omni-

OB-
against, in the way of, over, very

OMNI-
all

*obdurate, obfuscate, obligation, obliterate, obnoxious, obsess,
obsequious, obstacle, obstinate, obtrude, obviate,
omnipotent, omnipresent, omniscient, omnivorous*

Word Definitions

obdurate **adj.** stubbornly refusing to change one's opinion or course of action
"Scrooge was an <u>obdurate</u> miser who wouldn't part willingly with a penny, until he was visited by Marley's ghost and three other specters."
obduracy (n.)
obdurare to be hard; to persist: *ob-* against + *durare* to harden

obfuscate **v.** to render obscure or unintelligible
"My view of the road was <u>obfuscated</u> by rain and fog."
obfuscation (n.), obfuscatory (adj.)
obfuscare to darken: *ob-* (expressing intensity) + *fuscare* to darken

obligation **n.** an act or course of action to which a person is legally or morally bound
"It once was an <u>obligation</u> for all men to serve in the military."
oblige (v.)
obligare to bind, to oblige: *ob-* very + *ligare* to bind

obliterate **v.** to destroy utterly; to wipe out; erase
"After she broke his heart, he tried to <u>obliterate</u> all reminders of her."
obliteration (n.)
obliterare to cause to be forgotten, to strike out: *ob-* against + *littera* letter, something written

LESSON XIV: OB-, OMNI-

obnoxious   **adj.** extremely unpleasant or annoying
"The boy's obnoxious antics got on his mother's nerves."
obnoxius exposed to harm; guilty: *ob-* in the way of + *noxa* harm, crime

obsequious   **adj.** obedient or attentive to an excessive or servile degree
"The duke's behavior toward the emperor was nauseatingly obsequious."
obsequi to follow, to comply with: *ob-* very + *sequor* to follow

obsess   **v.** to be continually preoccupied with (something or someone)
"Ahab was so obsessed with capturing Moby Dick that he endangered the lives of his crew."
obsession (n.)
obsidere to besiege or occupy: *ob-* very + *sidere* to settle (on something)

obstacle   **n.** a thing that blocks one's way or hinders progress
"For the billionaire, cost was no obstacle to obtaining every luxury."
obstare to impede or oppose: *ob-* against + *stare* to stand firm

obstinate   **adj.** difficult to overcome or change; stubborn
"The obstinate mule refused to budge."
obstinacy (n.)
obstinare to persist: *ob-* very + *stare* to stand firm (variant form)

obtrude   **v.** to impose or force oneself on others; to thrust outward
"The rude guest obtruded on his host's privacy."
obtrusion (n.)
obtrudere to thrust, to shove: *ob-* against + *trudere* to push

obviate   **v.** to remove (a need or difficulty); to make unnecessary
"She planned to turn him down tactfully the next time he asked for a date, but he never called, obviating the need to reject him."
obviation (n.)
obviare to prevent: *ob-* against + *via* way, road, journey

omnipotent   **adj.** having absolute power
"The 'Almighty,' as the name implies, is an omnipotent god."
omnipotence (n.)
omnipotent all-powerful: *omni-* all + *potestas* power, rule, strength

omnipresent   **adj.** present everywhere simultaneously
"With a McDonald's in every town, the franchise seems omnipresent."
omnipresence (n.)
omnipraesens omnipresent: *omni-* all + *praesens* present, at hand

omniscient   **adj.** knowing everything
"An omniscient god is aware of even the smallest sin or kindness."
omniscience (n.)
omniscient all-knowing: *omni-* all + *scire* to know, to understand

omnivorous   **adj.** eating food of both plant and animal origin
"Humans are omnivorous, eating both plants and animals."
omnivore (n.) omni- all + *vorare* to eat

LESSON XIV: OB-, OMNI-

EXERCISE A

Fill in the blanks in the sentences below with the correct form of a word in the scroll above.

1. Her mother reminded Nicole that she could _____ a massive cleaning by tidying her bedroom each day.

2. Derek spent his vacation in Spain _____ over his upcoming exams, instead of enjoying the attractions and museums.

3. The oracle at Delphi was considered _____ because she could prophesy accurately.

4. A detonated atomic bomb can _____ an entire city.

5. Martin thought he was bringing the gospel of Christ to the unenlightened, but those to whom he preached felt he was _____ his opinions on them.

6. Christians generally believe God is _____ and therefore has the power to answer their prayers.

7. The _____ employee repeatedly flattered his boss to the point of being servile.

8. The nearby pulp and paper mill gave off an _____ odor, so the town was unable to attract tourists, despite its beautiful location and historic architecture.

9. Speed skiers are adept at averting the natural and artificial _____ on black diamond trails.

10. The truth was _____ by conflicting news reports.

11. The _____ man kept insisting that his family go to the movies, even though they would have preferred a trip to the mall.

12. He didn't want to serve on the budget committee, but felt his service was an _____ he couldn't avoid.

13. Although he traveled in hopes of leaving his troubles behind, he found they were _____ .

14. Eminem's _____ refusal to remove the controversial lyrics from his songs won him the support of some in the music industry and the rancor of others.

15. Though Susan simply meant that John was not a vegetarian, everyone found it funny that she called him _____ because he seemed to eat everything in sight.

EXERCISE B

Match the word with the letter of its definition.

1. obdurate
2. obfuscate
3. obligation
4. obliterate
5. obnoxious
6. obsess
7. obsequious
8. obstacle
9. obstinate
10. obtrude
11. obviate
12. omnipotent
13. omnipresent
14. omniscient
15. omnivorous

a) extremely unpleasant
b) make unclear; confuse
c) having absolute power
d) course of action to which a person is bound
e) knowing everything
f) overly servile
g) stubborn or unyielding
h) to utterly destroy
i) stubborn; not easily overcome
j) present everywhere at the same time
k) to impose
l) something that impedes progress
m) to think about constantly
n) to remove or make unnecessary
o) eating food of both plant and animal origin

EXERCISE C

Circle the letter of the definition that best fits the meaning of the bold-faced word.

1. **obdurate**
   a. agreeing to improve
   b. forcing to change
   c. seemingly hungry
   d. stubbornly refusing to change
   e. impeding progress

2. **obfuscate**
   a. confuse
   b. think about
   c. question
   d. demand
   e. force

3. **obligation**
   a. triumph
   b. commitment
   c. oversight
   d. question
   e. junction

4. **obliterate**
   a. interrogate
   b. take apart
   c. build over ruins
   d. ridicule
   e. utterly destroy

LESSON XIV: OB-, OMNI-

5. **obnoxious**
   a. sweet smelling
   b. full of fumes
   c. extremely unpleasant
   d. fawning
   e. very pleasant

6. **obsess**
   a. confuse a situation
   b. doubt the truth
   c. think about constantly
   d. demand whole-heartedly
   e. refuse to think about

7. **obsequious**
   a. sickeningly respectful
   b. differing greatly
   c. rudely dismissive
   d. clueless
   e. disinterested

8. **obstacle**
   a. large sign
   b. object that impedes
   c. element of a whole
   d. stunning sensation
   e. mud puddle

9. **obstinate**
   a. overly demanding
   b. emotional, especially quick to anger
   c. dismissive or rude
   d. difficult to overcome or change
   e. kind, caring

10. **obtrude**
    a. lose track of
    b. confuse
    c. question
    d. impose
    e. destroy

11. **obviate**
    a. make unnecessary
    b. become angry
    c. exclude from a group
    d. feel depressed
    e. refuse to think about

12. **omnipotent**
    a. eating potent foods
    b. labeling potable water
    c. having unlimited or enormous power
    d. being electrified
    e. having no control

13. **omnipresent**
    a. giving presents and gifts
    b. going everywhere
    c. knowing the time
    d. present everywhere at the same time
    e. knowing everything

14. **omniscient**
    a. knowing nothing
    b. caring about everything
    c. knowing everything
    d. wondering about everything
    e. questioning everything

15. **omnivorous**
    a. feeding on only plants
    b. eating food of both plant and animal origin
    c. overeating
    d. eating only meat
    e. caring little about food

LESSON XIV: OB-, OMNI-

Exercise D

Solve the crossword puzzle.

Across
1. An act or course of action to which a person is legally or morally bound. 2. Present everywhere at the same time. 3. A thing that blocks one's way or hinders progress. 5. Knowing everything. 6. Extremely unpleasant or annoying. 7. To impose or force (something) on someone; to thrust out. 8. To remove (a need or difficulty); to avoid; to prevent. 9. Stubbornly refusing to change one's opinion or course of action. 10. Difficult to overcome or change; stubborn

Down
1. Obedient or attentive to an excessive or servile degree. 3. To destroy utterly; to wipe out; erase. 4. To preoccupy continually. 5. Feeding on a variety of food of both plant and animal origin. 6. Having unlimited or very great power. 10. To make unclear or unintelligible.

Lesson XV:
Per-

PER-
through, completely

percolate, perfection, perforate, permeable, permission, permutation, pernicious, perpetrate, perplex, persevere, perspective, perspicacious, perspire, pertinent, perturb

Word Definitions

percolate v. to filter through a porous substance; to brew by percolation
"The water gradually <u>percolated</u> into the sand."
percolation (n.)
percolare to strain through: *per-* through + *colare* to filter

perfection n. the action, process, or condition of excellence or flawlessness
"A royal flush represents <u>perfection</u> in a poker hand."
perfect (v./adj.)
perficere to finish: *per-* completely + *facere* to do

perforate v. to pierce and make a hole or holes in
"Band-Aids are <u>perforated</u> with tiny holes to allow air flow."
perforation (adj.)
perforare to pierce through: *per-* completely + *forare* to pierce

permeable adj. (of a material or membrane) allowing liquids or gas to pass through
"Cells allow some liquids to pass through their <u>permeable</u> walls."
permeare to pass through: *per-* completely + *meare* to pass, to travel

LESSON XV: PER-

permission
    n. consent, authorization
"Security clearances include permission to see classified data."
permit (v.)
permittere to allow (through): *per-* completely + *mittere* to release, to send

permutation
    n. one of several possible ways in which a set or number of things can be ordered or arranged
"Three choices of bread and two of drinks allow six permutations of bread and drink."
permutate (v.)
permutare to change completely: *per-* completely + *mutare* to change

pernicious
    adj. having a very harmful effect
"For those who are allergic to it, poison ivy is a pernicious plant."
perniciosus destructive < *pernicies* ruin: *per-* completely + *nex, necis* violent death

perpetuate
    v. to cause to continue; to preserve for future use or in memory
"Jim's refusal to read aloud in class perpetuated the rumor that he was illiterate."
perpetuity (n.), perpetuance (n.), perpetuation (n.)
perpetuare to make permanent < *perpetuus* continuing, uninterrupted

perplex
    v. to cause (someone) to feel baffled
"Hieroglyphs perplexed scholars until the Rosetta Stone was discovered."
perplexus entangled: *per-* thoroughly + *plexus* < *plectere* to entwine

persevere
    v. to continue a course of action despite difficulty or scant chance of success
"Because the tortoise persevered, he beat the hare."
perseverance (n.)
perseverare to persist < *perseverus* very strict: *per-* thoroughly + *severus* severe

perspective
    n. an artistic technique for representing distance and three-dimensional objects on a flat surface; a view or prospect; a point of view (on a topic)
"The use of perspective in Renaissance drawing gave an appearance of depth and dimension."
perspicere to examine closely: *per-* thoroughly + *specere* to look

perspicacious
    adj. having a ready insight into and understanding of (ideas, things)
"Sherlock Holmes was perspicacious in finding and interpreting clues."
perspicacity (n.)
perspicere to examine closely: *per-* thoroughly + *specere* to look

perspire
    v. to sweat through the pores of the skin
"My grandmother used to say, 'Horses sweat, men perspire, and women glow.'"
perspiration (n.)
perspirare to breathe through; to perspire: *per-* through + *spirare* to breathe

LESSON XV: PER-

pertinent   **adj.** relevant or applicable to a particular matter
"Khalid's remarks are always pertinent and to the point."
pertinere to relate to: *per-* thoroughly + *tenere* to possess, to comprehend

perturb   **v.** to make anxious or unsettled
"The boy's parents were perturbed by his low test grades."
perturbare to confuse or trouble: *per-* completely + *turbare* to agitate

EXERCISE A

Fill in the blanks in the sentences below with the correct form of a word in the scroll above.

1. Water flowed through the _____ net, but most fish and shellfish were too large to fit through the tiny holes.

2. Atomic weapons are among the most _____ inventions of the twentieth century.

3. A marathon is a test not only of the athletes' physical conditions, but also their willingness to _____ through pain and exhaustion.

4. When it rains, water _____ through the soil to the water table.

5. The retired general was sought out by presidents of both parties for his knowledge and _____ advice.

6. The documentary film _____ Idi Amin's reputation as an erratic, narcissistic and mentally ill dictator.

7. Anton was _____ by Susan's cutting remark.

8. The hole punch _____ the paper so it could be put in the binder.

9. Dan's comment about medieval warfare was not _____ to the class discussion about modern politics.

10. *Beowulf*, written in Old English, _____ Delores until she became more familiar with the arcane language.

11. The manager planned to try different _____ of the lineup until he found a successful batting order.

12. People _____ in hot weather because the evaporation of sweat from the skin cools the body.

121

LESSON XV: PER-

13. From Steve's _____, the ball appeared to land in bounds, but the line judge declared it out.

14. Some people wish to achieve only mediocrity, while others strive for _____.

15. After much discussion, we were given _____ to attend a late-night concert in the city.

EXERCISE B

Match the word with the letter of its definition.

1. **percolate**
2. **perfection**
3. **perforate**
4. **permeable**
5. **permission**
6. **permutation**
7. **pernicious**
8. **perpetuate**
9. **perplex**
10. **persevere**
11. **perspective**
12. **perspicacious**
13. **perspire**
14. **pertinent**
15. **perturb**

a) coffee machine
b) tending to cause great harm or injury
c) capable of being passed through
d) persist in a task against the odds
e) acutely perceptive or discerning
f) change in the order of something
g) connected with a specific matter; relevant
h) confuse or cause uncertainty
i) upset or greatly disturb
j) make a hole in; pierce
k) sweat
l) point of view
m) to cause to continue
n) flawless excellence
o) authorization

EXERCISE C

Circle the letter of the definition which best fits the meaning of the bold-faced word.

1. **percolate**
   a. sort pages
   b. small grater
   c. grab attention
   d. seep through
   e. cause trouble

2. **perfection**
   a. mirror image
   b. flawless excellence
   c. formal procedure
   d. coffee-maker
   e. alternate version

LESSON XV: PER-

3. **perforate**
   a. fill in a hole
   b. cover up
   c. hide
   d. dig a hole
   e. make a hole in; pierce

4. **permeable**
   a. capable of being passed through
   b. waterproof
   c. solid
   d. vague
   e. uninteresting; dull

5. **permission**
   a. justification
   b. failure
   c. allowance
   d. consent, authorization
   e. freedom

6. **permutation**
   a. constructing the front of
   b. proceeding with care
   c. alternating the installation of
   d. imagining the image of
   e. change in the order or contents of something

7. **pernicious**
   a. influential
   b. capable of inspiring
   c. tending to cause boredom
   d. avoiding danger
   e. causing great harm or injury

8. **perpetuate**
   a. fail to complete
   b. start and stop
   c. enjoy
   d. cause to continue
   e. do harm to

9. **perplex**
   a. carefully think about
   b. understand or discern
   c. provoke ridicule or scorn
   d. confuse or cause uncertainty
   e. tease mercilessly

10. **persevere**
    a. give up
    b. smile at
    c. persist despite poor odds
    d. lose hope for the future
    e. work

11. **perspective**
    a. point of view or aspect
    b. the ability to see into the future
    c. common interest
    d. distraction
    e. joke

12. **perspicacious**
    a. vague
    b. acutely perceptive
    c. different
    d. mysterious; secretive
    e. very small

13. **perspire**
    a. sweat
    b. laugh
    c. inspire
    d. observe
    e. write

14. **pertinent**
    a. unrelated to each other
    b. especially important
    c. attracted to each other
    d. causing distress
    e. relevant to a specific matter

15. **perturb**
    a. quiet down
    b. cause peace
    c. upset or disturb greatly
    d. laugh at
    e. enjoy a meal

Exercise D

Solve the crossword puzzle.

Across
1. To make anxious or unsettled. 2. To pierce and make a hole or holes in. 4. To cause (someone) to feel baffled. 6. Consent, authorization. 8. To give out sweat through the pores of the skin. 10. The art of representing three-dimensional objects on a two-dimensional surface; a view or prospect; a particular way of regarding something. 11. Having a ready insight into and understanding of things.

Down
1. Each of several possible ways in which a set or number of things can be ordered or arranged. 3. Relevant or applicable to a particular matter. 4. Having a harmful effect. 5. To continue in a course of action in spite of difficulty or with little or no indication of success. 6. To cause to continue indefinitely. 8. (Of a material or membrane) allowing liquids or gas to pass through it. 9. The action, process, or condition of perfecting or being perfect.

Lesson XVI:
Post, Pre-, Prim-

POST
after

PRE-
before

PRIM-
first

posterity, posthumous, postmortem, postpone, postscript,
preamble, precept, preclude, precocious, prediction, prefabricated,
premature, premeditated, presume, pretentious,
primal, primary, primate, primeval, primogeniture

Word Definitions

posterity
n. future generations; all the descendants of one person
"Public libraries were Franklin's gift to posterity."
posterus coming after; descendants < *post* after, behind

posthumous
adj. occurring, awarded, or appearing after the death of (someone)
"The novel was published posthumously."
postumus final: *post* after + *humus* ground, soil < *humare* to bury

postmortem
n. a medical examination to determine the cause of death; an autopsy; analysis of a failure
adj. done after death
"The coroner asked a trauma surgeon to help him with the postmortem."
post after + *mortem* death; corpse

postpone
v. to put off until later (something scheduled or due)
"The cross-examination was postponed after the witness fell ill."
postponere to set aside: *post* after + *ponere* to place

postscript
n. an additional remark at the end of a letter; a brief sequel
"A postscript added at the bottom of a letter is abbreviated: P.S."
postscribere to write under: *post* after + *scribere* to write

LESSON XVI: POST, PRE-, PRIM-

preamble	**n.** a preliminary statement, an introduction "The stiff breeze was a mere preamble to the subsequent gale." *praeambulus* going before: *prae-* before + *ambulare* to walk
precept	**n.** a general rule for behavior or thought "The Golden Rule is a precept found in many religions." *praecipere* to teach; to take in advance: *prae-* before + *capere* to take
preclude	**v.** to prevent (something) from happening or (someone) from doing something "Winter and a scorched earth policy precluded a victory by Napoleon." *preclusion (n.)* *praecludere* to close, to block: *prae-* before + *claudere* to shut
precocious	**adj.** demonstrating advanced abilities at an early age *precocity/precociousness (n.)* "The precocious J. S. Mill could read Latin and Greek by age four." *pre-* before + *coquere* to cook; to mature
prediction	**n.** a forecast "The Oracle of Delphi issued strange predictions of future events." *predict (v.)* *praedicere* to say beforehand: *prae-* before + *dicere* to say
prefabricated	**adj.** made in sections for assembly on site "Prefabricated modules are used to construct the space station." *prefabricate (v.)* *pre-* before + *fabricare* to make < *fabrica* craft
premature	**adj.** occurring or done before the proper time "Without awaiting all the facts, one might make a premature judgment." *prematurity (n.)* *praematurus* very early, premature: *prae-* before + *maturus* ripe
premeditated	**adj.** thought out or planned beforehand "Murder planned in advance is considered premeditated." *premeditation (n.)* *praemeditari* to consider in advance: *prae-* before + *meditari* to think out
presume	**v.** to suppose (something) is true or take it for granted; to venture (to do something) "Dewey was the presumed victor, but in the end Truman won." *presumptuous (adj.), presumption (n.)* *praesumere* to anticipate; to take for granted: *prae-* before + *sumere* to take
pretentious	**adj.** affecting greater importance or merit than one possesses "Hoping to impress, the pretentious preppie spoke with an English accent." *pretentiousness (n.)* *praetendere* to stretch forth; to claim: *prae-* before + *tendere* to stretch
primal	**adj.** relating to an early stage in evolutionary development "Food, self-preservation, and sex are primal human urges." *primus* first

primary	**adj.** of chief importance, principal; earliest in time or order "His job was the family's primary means of support." *primarius* of the first rank; distinguished < *primus* first
primate	**n.** a mammal of the order including humans, monkeys and gorillas; an archbishop or bishop who is more important than others in a region "Unlike our close primate relatives, we humans walk upright." *primas* of the highest rank < *primus* first
primeval	**adj.** from earliest history "Eons of pressure turned primeval vegetation into coal and petroleum." *primus* first
primogeniture	**n.** the state of being the firstborn child; the practice of the eldest son inheriting a father's property "Primogeniture prevented the break-up of family estates." *primogenitura* right of the first-born child: *primo-* at first + *genitura* birth < *gignere* to beget

EXERCISE A

Fill in the blanks in the sentences below with the correct form of a word in the scroll above.

1. Every American schoolchild knows the opening words to the _____ of the U.S. Constitution: "We the people of the United States."

2. Although it had begun to drizzle, the referee was reluctant to _____ the game because the fans had already arrived.

3. Mike's _____ that *Chicago* would not win anything at the Academy Awards appeared foolish when the movie won seven Oscars, including "Best Picture."

4. The World War II veteran died before he could be awarded the Purple Heart, but his family accepted the _____ medal on his behalf.

5. The Royal Guard, Buckingham Palace, and the entire institution of the British monarchy may seem _____ to Americans, but they are a source of great pride for many British citizens.

6. Johnny Depp has long reveled in the Hollywood spotlight, but he now understands that his _____ responsibility is as a father to his children.

7. Scientists point to fossils of _____ life forms as evidence for the theory of evolution.

LESSON XVI: POST, PRE-, PRIM-

8. Amanda's _____ meant she received the undivided attention of her parents; her younger siblings were almost neglected by comparison.

9. The Golden Rule states "Do unto others as you would have them do unto you." The entire world should live by this simple _____.

10. Indiana Jones was able to decipher the cryptic letter when he realized that the seemingly innocuous _____, "P. S. Don't forget to feed the cat," was actually a coded message referring to the Nazis on his trail.

11. When Mozart began to display his talents as a musical prodigy at an incredibly young age, his parents were quick to seek proper training for the _____ boy.

12. Recognizing his limitations as a craftsman, Homer bought a _____ swing set for his children.

13. In *Lord of the Flies*, boys deserted on an island abandon all civilized rules and succumb to _____ urges and instincts.

14. Research indicates that most thefts on college campuses are not _____; they are usually "crimes of opportunity," committed when the potential thief sees an unattended laptop or stereo.

15. After the complete failure of the project, the staff conducted a _____ meeting to analyze the causes.

16. Most bestselling books are forgotten a few months or years after publication, but true classics are valued by _____.

17. When the chimp escaped from the zoo, it took the animal control officer weeks to locate the resourceful _____, who slept in trees and scavenged from garbage cans while enjoying her newfound freedom.

18. Starring in *The Lord of the Rings* trilogy _____ actor Elijah Wood from appearing in any other movies for the entire, three-year production period.

19. With no physical description or photo to go by, Hank could only _____ that the woman sitting alone at a table in Starbucks was his arranged date.

20. The unexpectedly _____ ageing of her skin led the woman to seek cosmetic surgery.

LESSON XVI: POST, PRE-, PRIM-

EXERCISE B

Match the word with the letter of its definition;

1. posterity
2. posthumous
3. postmortem
4. postpone
5. postscript
6. preamble
7. precept
8. preclude
9. precocious
10. prediction
11. prefabricated
12. premature
13. premeditated
14. presume
15. pretentious
16. primal
17. primary
18. primates
19. primeval
20. primogeniture

a) put off to a later time
b) make an assumption
c) medical exam after death
d) introduction to a speech or document
e) additional message after signature in a letter
f) humans, apes, and monkeys
g) first in rank or importance
h) basic rule of conduct
i) statement forecasting the future
j) basic, primitive
k) made in sections for quick assembly
l) from the earliest ages of earth
m) unusually intelligent or skilled at a young age
n) future generations
o) condition of being the first born child
p) before the proper time
q) make impossible; prevent
r) awarded or appearing after death
s) planned beforehand
t) pretending increased importance or stature

EXERCISE C

Circle the letter of the definition which best fits the meaning of the bold-faced word.

1. **posterity**
   a. ancestors
   b. brotherhood
   c. old age
   d. the future
   e. future generations

2. **posthumous**
   a. occurring after death
   b. occurring before birth
   c. evoking laughter
   d. funereal
   e. relating to the past

LESSON XVI: POST, PRE-, PRIM-

3. **postmortem**
   a. period of time preceding death
   b. state of mourning
   c. pregnancy
   d. consequence
   e. autopsy

4. **postpone**
   a. wander off
   b. lengthen
   c. exercise
   d. develop prematurely
   e. put off to a later time

5. **postscript**
   a. introduction to a letter
   b. ending to a story
   c. additional text after the signature in a letter
   d. offhand comment
   e. short story

6. **preamble**
   a. conclusion
   b. discussion
   c. introduction
   d. signature
   e. laugh

7. **precept**
   a. instance of confusion
   b. problem
   c. rule of conduct
   d. boundary
   e. dignitary, a noble

8. **preclude**
   a. prevent
   b. start
   c. postpone
   d. destroy
   e. build

9. **precocious**
   a. old and wise
   b. slow to react
   c. so introspective as to be oblivious to the surrounding world
   d. unfortunate or hopeless
   e. unusually intelligent or skilled at a young age

10. **prediction**
    a. the quiet period before a speech
    b. a qualifying statement
    c. state of confusion
    d. issue in a legal argument
    e. a prophecy

11. **prefabricated**
    a. made in sections for quick assembly
    b. made from scratch
    c. imagined; not real
    d. spoiled or rotten
    e. dishonest; untrustworthy

12. **premature**
    a. reverting back to an original state
    b. before the proper time
    c. uncertain
    d. controversial
    e. straying from the ordinary

13. **premeditated**
    a. unprepared and unskilled
    b. unchanged, steady
    c. without thought; instinctive
    d. peaceful and spiritual
    e. planned beforehand

14. **presume**
    a. make an assumption
    b. prove an assertion
    c. experiment with
    d. take control of
    e. deceive

LESSON XVI: POST, PRE-, PRIM-

15. **pretentious**
    a. tending to be annoying
    b. relating to money
    c. stretching very thin
    d. having great power and responsibility
    e. attempting to assume increased importance or stature

16. **primal**
    a. futuristic
    b. basic, primitive
    c. past events
    d. evil, bad
    e. automatic, not requiring thought

17. **primary**
    a. of the earliest era of the earth
    b. first in order, time, or place
    c. unimportant, useless
    d. intelligent, quick-witted
    e. an ordinal number

18. **primate**
    a. close friend or family member
    b. earliest form of life found on earth
    c. opponent; adversary
    d. first love
    e. ape or monkey

19. **primeval**
    a. of the earliest eras on Earth
    b. of scientific inquiry
    c. of a temporary nature
    d. of an awesome size
    e. of a just cause

20. **primogeniture**
    a. condition of being the firstborn child
    b. condition of being an only child
    c. large amount of money spent
    d. condition of being at a physical peak
    e. act of forgiveness

Exercise D

Solve the crossword puzzle:

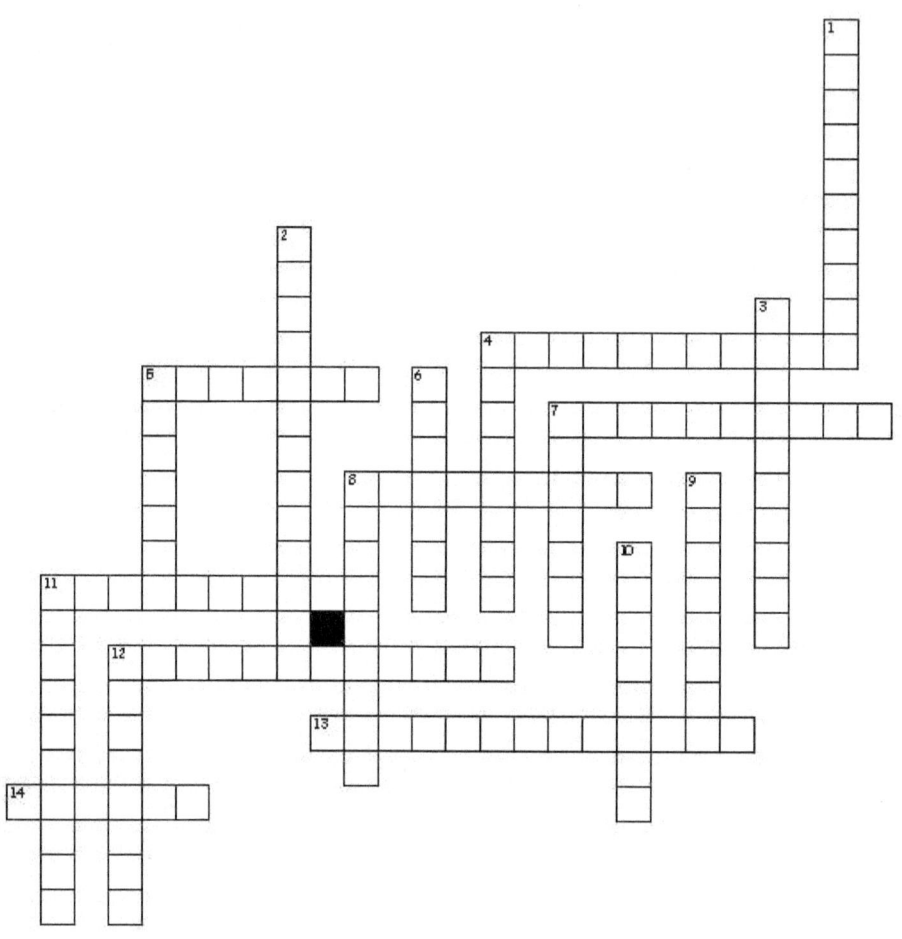

Across
4. Affecting greater status or merit than one actually possesses. 5. Of chief importance, principal; earliest in time or order. 7. A forecast. 8. Future generations. 11. A medical examination of a dead body to determine the cause of death. 12. Thought out or planned beforehand. 13. The state of being the firstborn child; the practice of the eldest son inheriting a father's property. 14. Relating to an early stage in evolutionary development.

Down
1. Having developed certain abilities or inclinations in childhood. 2. Manufactured for quick assembly on site. 3. Occurring, awarded, or appearing after the death of the originator. 4. Of the earliest time in history. 5. A general rule regulating behavior or thought. 6. To assume or take for granted. 7. The order of mammals including humans, monkeys and apes. 8. Occurring or done before the proper time. 9. To put off until later. 10. To prevent (something) from happening or (someone) from doing something. 11. An additional remark at the end of a letter. 12. A preliminary statement.

Test 3

1. "Then silent, scarcely uttering an <u>interjection</u> of admiration, they gazed, they contemplated."

   Round The Moon by Jules Verne

   (a) question   (b) phrase   (c) grammar   (d) exclamation   (e) explanation

2. "It was the only battle which I have ever witnessed, the only battle-field I ever trod while the battle was raging; <u>internecine</u> war; the red republicans on the one hand, and the black imperialists on the other."

   Walden by Henry David Thoreau

   (a) pointless   (b) internal   (c) foreign   (d) harmful   (e) negative

3. "During this <u>interregnum</u> we begin a very original and interesting series of maneuvers."

   War and Peace by Leo Tolstoy

   (a) contest   (b) kingly lifestyle   (c) period between governments
   (d) period of continuity   (e) period of hostility

4. "The light in the room found its way outward through the <u>interstices</u> of closed wooden shutters."

   The Two Destinies by Wilkie Collins

   (a) cracks   (b) large spaces   (c) supports   (d) edges   (e) louvers

5. "I was half out of bed, and Duncan had been hanging at the elbow of these fighting cocks, ready to <u>intervene</u> upon the least occasion."

   Kidnapped by Robert Louis Stevenson

   (a) participate   (b) disapprove   (c) surprise   (d) alter   (e) step in

6. " An aunt of my father's, and consequently a great-aunt of mine, of whom I shall have more to relate by and by, was the principal magnate of our family."
David Copperfield by Charles Dickens

   (a) strong attraction   (b) matriarch   (c) powerful person   (d) money saver
   (e) problem solver

7. "Two orders he had given at the first sign of an utterly unforeseen onset; after that the magnitude of his mistake seemed to have overwhelmed him."
The Mirror of the Sea by Joseph Conrad

   (a) intention   (b) attitude   (c) quality   (d) extent   (e) decision

8. "I watched her a few moments with a feeling of malevolent gratification; then, moving towards the door, I calmly asked if she had anything more to say."
The Tenant of Wildfell Hall by Anne Bronte

   (a) malicious   (b) evident   (c) grateful   (d) entertaining   (e) faithful

9. "As yet she felt none of the malign consequences of the self-denial she was about to exert."
Autobiography of a Pocket-Handkerchief by James Fenimore Cooper

   (a) kind   (b) mischievous   (c) evil   (d) criminal   (e) helpful

10. "The little flat was hot and stuffy under the August sun, and from the road beat up a malodorous sultriness."
Of Human Bondage by Somerset Maugham

    (a) loud   (b) sweet   (c) quiet   (d) stinking   (e) unpleasant

11. "They were greatly shocked--even the obdurate heart of Sir Edward and the insensible one of Augusta, were touched with sorrow by the unhappy tale."
Love and Friendship by Jane Austen

    (a) progressive   (b) hardened   (c) hungry   (d) improving   (e) unhappy

12. "And there was Silver, sitting back almost out of the firelight, but eating heartily, prompt to spring forward when anything was wanted, even joining quietly in our laughter--the same bland, polite, obsequious seaman of the voyage out."
Treasure Island by Robert Louis Stevenson

    (a) servile   (b) differing   (c) comely   (d) sincere   (e) demanding

13. "No--there is something else concerning which I should like to write to you, but am afraid to obtrude upon your notice."
Poor Folk by Fyodor Dostoyevsky

    (a) destroy   (b) impose   (c) confuse   (d) question   (e) avoid

14. "The difficulty thus placed in my way I determined to obviate in the following manner."
Typee by Herman Melville

    (a) counteract   (b) object   (c) remove   (d) control   (e) label

15. "It appeared to be omniscient and omnipotent, and yet was neither seen nor heard."
A Study In Scarlet by Sir Arthur Conan Doyle

    (a) all powerful   (b) all controlling   (c) all present   (d) all giving
    (e) all knowing

16. "It macerates its opium and percolates its own laudanum and paregoric."
The Four Million by O. Henry

    (a) pierces   (b) mirrors   (c) alternates   (d) brews   (e) attends to

17. "The substance of the wall seemed as permeable and yielding as light."
White Fang by Jack London

    (a) waterproof   (b) penetrable   (c) vague
    (d) substantial   (e) hidden

18. "Their reputation, as holders of mystic and pernicious principles, having spread before them, the Puritans early endeavored to banish, and to prevent the further intrusion of the rising sect."
From Twice Told Tales by Nathaniel Hawthorne

    (a) harmful   (b) frightening   (c) delightful   (d) disturbing   (e) deteriorating

19. "Certainly vain-glory helpeth to <u>perpetuate</u> a man's memory; and virtue was never so beholding to human nature, as it received his due at the second hand."
  The Essays by Sir Francis Bacon

    (a) fail (b) enjoy (c) prolong (d) complete (e) harm

20. "Not seeing his way to any <u>pertinent</u> answer, Mr. Glegg reverted to his porridge."
  The Mill on the Floss by George Eliot

    (a) unrelated (b) attractive (c) erroneous (d) relevant (e) secretive

21. "'Yes yes,' said Caderousse; and his eyes glistened at the thought of this <u>posthumous</u> revenge."
  The Count of Monte Cristo by Alexandre Dumas

    (a) off-putting (b) after death (c) premature (d) after birth (e) extended

22. "I don't want a religion that I put away with my Sunday clothes, and don't take out till the day comes round again; I want something to see and feel and live by day-by-day, and I hope you'll be one of the true ministers, who can teach by <u>precept</u> and example, how to get and keep it."
  An Old-Fashioned Girl by Louisa May Alcott

    (a) principle (b) boundary (c) introduction (d) problem (e) foresight

23. "Therefore, you would scarcely be interested in Kim's experiences as a St. Xavier's boy among two or three hundred <u>precocious</u> youths, most of whom had never seen the sea."
  Kim by Rudyard Kipling

    (a) viable (b) obvious (c) intelligent (d) unfortunate (e) introspective

24. "'My thesis is,' he says, 'that if we start with the supposition that there is only one <u>primal</u> stuff or material in the world, a stuff of which everything is composed, and if we call that stuff pure experience.'"
  The Analysis of Mind by Bertrand Russell

    (a) ultimate (b) evil (c) futuristic (d) fundamental (e) automatic

25. "The surrounding shores were beautiful with semitropical verdure, while in the distance the country rose from the ocean in hill and tableland, almost uniformly clothed by <u>primeval</u> forest."
  Tarzan of the Apes by Edgar Rice Burroughs

    (a) scientific (b) malevolent (c) temporary (d) ancient (e) closed

Lesson XVII:
Pro-

PRO-
forward, forth, on behalf of, in front of

> *procedure, proceed, procession, procrastinate, procure, prodigal, profane, proficient, profit, profuse, prohibit, prominent, pronounce, propensity, proponent, propulsion, prospect, protract, protrude, provoke*

Word Definitions

procedure
n. a series of steps for doing something
"He refused to follow the established surgical procedure because he had found a more effective method."
procedere advance: *pro-* forward + *cedere* to go

proceed
v. to begin or to continue a course of action; to move forward
"Socrates proceeded to drink the poison hemlock and quickly died."
procedere advance: *pro-* forward + *cedere* to go

procession
n. a number of people or vehicles moving forward in an orderly fashion; a parade
"The procession of job seekers continued throughout the day."
procedere advance: *pro-* forward + *cedere* to go

procrastinate
v. to delay or postpone an action
"The Procrastination Society always postpones its meetings."
procrastination (n.)
procrastinare to defer till the morning: *pro-* forward + *crastinus* belonging to the morning

LESSON XVII: PRO-

procure	**v.** to obtain; to buy or get something (for someone) "Michael Jackson procured the rights to nearly all of the Beatles' songs." *procurare* to take care of, to manage: *pro-* on behalf of + *curare* to care for
prodigal	**adj.** wastefully extravagant or lavish "In Aesop's fable, the grasshopper was prodigal, the ants thrifty." *prodigere* to drive away, to squander: *pro-* forth + *agere* to remove, to drive
profane	**adj.** secular rather than religious; vulgar or blasphemous "His profane speech scandalized the other church members." *profanity (n.)* *profanus* outside the temple, not sacred: *pro-* before + *fanum* temple
proficient	**adj.** competent or skilled in doing something "A proficient hitter, Maris batted 61 home runs in one season." *proficiency (n.)* *proficere* to make, to accomplish: *pro-* before + *facere* to make, to do
profit	**v.** to benefit from **n.** a financial gain; an advantage or benefit "What does a man profit if he gains wealth but loses his soul?" *profectus* profit, progress < *proficere* to make, to accomplish
profuse	**adj.** plentiful, abundant "The book was profusely illustrated, with more than 300 photographs." *profuseness (n.)* *profusus* lavish < *profundere* to pour out, to squander: *pro-* forth + *fundere* to pour
prohibit	**v.** to formally forbid by law, rule, etc.; to prevent "After the accident, he prohibited his son from driving the car." *prohibere* to hinder, to restrain: *pro-* in front + *habere* to hold
prominent	**adj.** particularly noticeable; important or famous; projecting "Cyrano de Bergerac had an enormous, prominent nose." *prominence (n.)* *prominere* to jut out: *pro-* forth + *minere* to jut, to threaten
pronounce	**v.** to make the sound of; to declare or announce; to make more obvious "The pastor pronounced the couple man and wife." *pronunciation (n.)* *pronuntiare* proclaim: *pro-* forth + *nuntiare* to announce < *nuntius* messenger
propensity	**n.** an inclination or tendency "Though bright, the student had a propensity to slack off." *propendere* to be inclined: *pro-* forward, down + *pendere* to hang
proponent	**n.** a person who advocates a theory, proposal, or project "A proponent is in favor of a thing; an opponent is against it." *proponere* to set forth: *pro-* forward + *ponere* to put

LESSON XVII: PRO-

propulsion	**n.** the act of driving or pushing forward; the source of such motion "Swim fins provide increased propulsion underwater." *propellere* to drive before (oneself): *pro-* forth + *pellere* to drive
prospect	**n.** the possibility or likelihood of some future event occurring; chances or opportunities for success; a view or vista "An orphan with no money, Pip had slim prospects." *prospicere* to look forward: *pro-* forward + *specere* to look at
protract	**v.** to prolong; to drag out "Let's not protract this meeting; it's not productive." *protraction (n.)* *protrahere* to prolong: *pro-* out + *trahere* to draw
protrude	**v.** to extend beyond or above a surface "A snorkel protruded from the smooth surface of the lake." *protrusion (n.)* *protrudere* to thrust forward: *pro-* forward, out + *trudere* to thrust
provoke	**v.** to cause something to happen; to annoy "Exposure to poison oak may provoke a rash." *provocative (adj.), provocation (n.)* *provocare* to challenge: *pro-* forth + *vocare* to call

EXERCISE A

Fill in the blanks in the sentences below with the correct form of a word in the scroll above

1. After the plane landed, the airline steward announced that we should _____ to the baggage claim.

2. Shop keepers generally _____ customers from eating or drinking inside so that patrons do not accidentally ruin the items for sale.

3. The _____ were excellent that the all-star high school athlete would be chosen for a college team.

4. The phrase "the _____ son " refers to the Biblical story of a young man who returned home repentant after wasting his money.

5. Our new neighbors are _____ of recycling and advocate composting as well.

6. Oftentimes during a funeral, a black hearse will lead a _____ of cars, which by law no vehicle other than an emergency vehicle may interrupt.

7. On the way home from school, Mike _____ Susan by grabbing her books and throwing them in bushes.

8. She gave the truck driver _____ thanks after he rescued her child.

9. Before jet _____ was invented, propeller planes were common.

10. Much to the dismay of most Americans, the decision of the 2000 presidential election was _____ for a month or more.

11. Since its founding, the company had been able to increase its _____ margin by 10% annually.

12. Pinocchio's nose _____ further each time he lied.

13. Please try to _____ your H's better so we can understand what you are saying.

14. Usually, all the town's most _____ citizens attend the celebrated Holiday Ball.

15. *Sacred and* _____ is a fascinating philosophical book, comparing and contrasting secular and religious life.

16. Admittedly it is tempting to _____; however, it is far better to complete your homework in a timely fashion.

17. The smooth bicycle tires' _____ to skid made riding in rainy weather even more dangerous.

18. The chef told his assistant to _____ 15 lbs. of broccoli at the market because it was the vegetable du jour.

19. Until carpenters become more _____ with new tools, they should use extreme care to prevent harm to themselves or damage to their projects.

20. The toddler's bedtime _____ included putting on his pajamas, brushing his teeth, and listening to a story.

EXERCISE B

Match the word with the letter of its definition.

1. **procedure**
2. **proceed**
3. **procession**
4. **procrastinate**
5. **procure**
6. **prodigal**
7. **profane**
8. **proficient**
9. **profit**
10. **profuse**
11. **prohibit**
12. **prominent**
13. **pronounce**
14. **propensity**
15. **proponent**
16. **propulsion**
17. **prospects**
18. **protract**
19. **protrude**
20. **provoke**

a) particularly noticeable
b) extend beyond or above a surface
c) secular rather than religious
d) chances or opportunities for success
e) forbid
f) person who advocates a theory or project
g) benefit financially
h) act of driving or pushing forward
i) inclination or tendency
j) obtain
k) way of doing something in steps
l) begin a course of action; move forward
m) deliberately annoy or anger
n) wastefully extravagant or lavish
o) delay or postpone a task
p) competent or skilled in doing something
q) make the sound of
r) plentiful; abundant
s) prolong; drag out
t) people or vehicles moving forward in an orderly fashion

EXERCISE C

Circle the letter of the definition that best fits the meaning of the bold-faced word.

1. **procedure**
   a. innovative method
   b. inconvenience
   c. steps for doing something
   d. proposal
   e. agreement

2. **proceed**
   a. move sideways
   b. move quickly
   c. move backward
   d. move forward
   e. prolong

3. **procession**
   a. changing positions
   b. a group moving forward in an orderly fashion
   c. becoming hysterical
   d. deliberately annoying
   e. a group moving around chaotically

4. **procrastinate**
   a. delay an action
   b. comprehend an action
   c. combine reactions
   d. benefit from an action
   e. justify one's actions

5. **procure**
   a. obtain
   b. let go
   c. be efficient
   d. stand together
   e. give away

6. **prodigal**
   a. kind
   b. frugal
   c. caring
   d. wasteful
   e. colorful

7. **profane**
   a. on time rather than late
   b. religious rather than secular
   c. tardy rather than early
   d. long rather than short
   e. secular rather than religious

8. **proficient**
   a. unskilled
   b. careful
   c. skilled
   d. careless
   e. useless

9. **profit**
   a. earn credits
   b. benefit financially
   c. work for a living
   d. spend money
   e. waste money

10. **profuse**
    a. plentiful
    b. stingy
    c. sloppy
    d. extended
    e. noisy

11. **prohibit**
    a. advocate
    b. extend the length
    c. refuse permission
    d. allow
    e. retire early

12. **prominent**
    a. forbidden, off limits
    b. particularly noticeable
    c. possibly occurring
    d. shy and retiring
    e. especially pretty

LESSON XVII: PRO-

13. pronounce
   a. make the sound of
   b. advocate
   c. propel forward
   d. prevent
   e. explore

14. propensity
   a. opportunity
   b. announcement
   c. incumbent
   d. inclination
   e. extension

15. proponent
   a. number of people
   b. official duty
   c. advocate
   d. airline steward
   e. skill

16. propulsion
   a. flying in circles
   b. driving or pushing forward
   c. projecting forward
   d. going backward
   e. walking forward

17. prospect
   a. chance for success
   b. prolonging the outcome
   c. delaying an action
   d. plenty, abundance
   e. possibility of failure

18. protract
   a. return; retrace
   b. delay; postpone
   c. prolong; drag out
   d. annoy; anger
   e. remove; take away

19. protrude
   a. withdraw under something
   b. move forward
   c. excel beyond expectation
   d. extend beyond or above a surface
   e. put away carefully

20. provoke
   a. excite a liking for
   b. casually announce
   c. deliberately annoy
   d. waste extravagantly
   e. postpone indefinitely

Exercise D

Solve the crossword puzzle.

Across
2. Wastefully extravagant or lavish. 3. To annoy or anger deliberately. 4. The act of driving or pushing forward; the source of such motion. 5. To begin a course of action; to move forward. 8. Steps for accomplishing something. 11. To forbid. 13. To make the sound of; to declare or announce; to make more obvious. 15. To delay or postpone an action. 16. To extend beyond or above a surface.

Down
1. To obtain. 2. Particularly noticeable; important or famous; projecting. 3. The possibility or likelihood of some future event occurring; chance or opportunity for success. 6. Competent or skilled in doing or using something. 7. An inclination or tendency. 8. Plentiful, abundant. 9. To benefit from. 10. Secular rather than religious; blasphemous. 12. A person who advocates a theory, proposal, or project. 14. To prolong; to drag out. 15. A number of people or vehicles moving forward in an orderly fashion.

Lesson XVIII:
Re-, Retro-

RE-
back, again

recite, recline, reconcile, recognize, refute, reimburse, reiterate, renown, repatriate, repose, reticent, retort, retroactive, retrograde, retrospect

Word Definitions

recite	**v.** to repeat aloud from memory; to state in order "Children are often required to <u>recite</u> poems in school." *recitation (n.)* *recitare* to read out: *re-* back, again + *citare* to cite, to quote
recline	**v.** to lean against or lie back in a relaxed manner "He <u>reclined</u> on the bench, smoking and studying her insolently." *reclining (adj.)* *reclinare* to bend back: *re-* back + *clinare* to bend
recognize	**v.** to identify as already known; to acknowledge "China does not <u>recognize</u> Taiwan as a sovereign country." *recognition (n.)* *recognoscere* to know again, to recall: *re-* again + *cognoscere* to learn
reconcile	**v.** to restore friendly relations between; to bring into agreement "I can't <u>reconcile</u> my checking account with my bank statement." *reconciliation (n.), reconciliatory (adj.)* *reconciliare* to restore, to reconcile: *re-* again + *conciliare* to bring together

145

refute	**v.** to prove to be wrong; to rebut "Galileo's observations <u>refuted</u> the idea of an earth-centered cosmos." *refutation (n.), refutable (adj.)* *refutare* to repel, to rebut, to refute
reimburse	**v.** to repay "Employee business expenses are <u>reimbursed</u> by the company." *reimbursement (n.)* *re-* again + *im-* into + *bursa* purse, funds
reiterate	**v.** to say something again; to restate "I said it before and I now <u>reiterate</u>: 'No new taxes!'" *reiteration (n.)* *reiterare* to go over again: *re-* (expressing repetition) + *iterare* to do again
renown	**n.** fame "Her <u>renown</u> made it impossible for her to dine out quietly." *renowned (adj.)* *re-* again + *nomen, nominis* name
repatriate	**v.** to send (someone) back to his or her own country; to go back to one's native land "The Tutsi refugees were eventually <u>repatriated</u> to Rwanda." *repatriation (n.)* *repatriare* to return to one's own country: *re-* back + *patria* native county
repose	**v.** to rest or sleep **n.** a state of restfulness or tranquility "Cleopatra <u>reposed</u> on a golden sofa in her barge." *repausare* to rest: *re-* again (expressing repetition) + *pausare* to pause
reticent	**adj.** not revealing one's thoughts or feelings readily "A <u>reticent</u> person may fear public speaking." *reticence (n.)* *reticere* to remain silent: *re-* again + *tacere* to be silent
retort	**v.** to say something sharp, angry, or witty in answer to a remark or accusation **n.** a sharp, angry, or witty reply "The English cannon fired first; French guns shot back in <u>retort</u>." *retorquere* to twist or bend back: *re-* back + *torquere* to twist, bend
retroactive	**adj.** taking effect starting at a date already past "Your raise will be <u>retroactive</u> to the beginning of the month." *retroactivity (n.)* *retro-* backwards + *activus* act
retrograde	**adj.** directed or moving backwards; reverting to an earlier or inferior condition "Astrologers say a planet is <u>retrograde</u> when the angle of view makes it appear to be moving backward in its usual course." *retro-* backward + *gradus* step or position

LESSON XVIII: RE-, RETRO-

retrospect   n. a survey or review of a past course of events
"At the time, it seemed a good idea. In <u>retrospect</u>, I see that it wasn't."
retrospective (adj.)
retro- backward + *prospectus* view

EXERCISE A

Fill in the blanks in the sentences below with the correct form of a word in the scroll above.

1. To qualify for the summer trip around the country, the students each had to memorize and _____ the Gettysburg Address to the class.

2. After the war was over, the U.S. insisted that its prisoners be _____.

3. While meditating in his new Zen garden, Alejandro was startled from his _____ by the sound of a traffic helicopter flying overhead.

4. The tax cut passed during the summer is _____ to January 1.

5. After the infield players once again committed errors in the ninth inning to lose the game, the manager _____ the importance of defense.

6. The banking customer _____ his lender in full for the loan.

7. After one of her colleagues was fired for questioning the company president, Suzanne was _____ to voice her concerns about the impending merger.

8. In _____, we might have been able to move in earlier, if we had not taken our vacation before I transferred to the new job.

9. At her tenth high school reunion, she _____ an old friend despite the classmate's changed appearance.

10. Chairs that _____ are far more comfortable than ones that do not.

11. When O. J. Simpson was accused of his wife's death, he angrily _____ that he was still looking for the real killer.

12. Janet _____ Bob's claims that she deliberately misled him, but no one believed her.

13. That vintage outfit is really _____.

LESSON XVIII: RE-, RETRO-

14. Although he was a pop star of great _____, Michael Jackson's reputation has been tarnished by allegations of pedophilia.

15. Despite a long-standing dispute, Dr. Dre and Easy E eventually _____ before the latter's premature death from AIDS.

EXERCISE B

Match the word with the letter of its definition.

1. **recite**
2. **recline**
3. **recognize**
4. **reconcile**
5. **refute**
6. **reimburse**
7. **reiterate**
8. **renown**
9. **repatriate**
10. **repose**
11. **reticent**
12. **retort**
13. **retroactive**
14. **retrograde**
15. **retrospect**

a) fame
b) to deny or disprove
c) directed or moving backwards
d) to repay
e) taking effect from a date in the past
f) to repeat for increased emphasis
g) to reply in an indignant manner
h) to send back to one's own country
i) to resolve differences, to make up
j) a review of a past course of events
k) to repeat by memory
l) to rest, relax
m) reserved, shy
n) to lean back or lie against
o) to identify as already known

EXERCISE C

Circle the letter of the definition that best fits the meaning of the bold-faced word.

1. **recite**
   a. improvise
   b. question someone's motives
   c. repeat for increased emphasis
   d. incite to riot
   e. perform from memory

2. **recline**
   a. fall backward
   b. quit abruptly
   c. lean back or lie down
   d. gape in amazement
   e. move forward

LESSON XVIII: RE-, RETRO-

3. **recognize**
   a. know again
   b. rehearse
   c. turn around
   d. come again
   e. consider carefully

4. **reconcile**
   a. explain
   b. resolve differences
   c. argue with
   d. make a judgment
   e. disapprove

5. **refute**
   a. deny
   b. relinquish command
   c. engage the enemy
   d. realize the importance of something
   e. reconsider

6. **reimburse**
   a. regain the trust of
   b. borrow money
   c. repay a loan
   d. break a promise
   e. deny payment

7. **reiterate**
   a. join a club
   b. repeat
   c. murmur
   d. coerce
   e. think about

8. **renown**
   a. wisdom
   b. honesty
   c. fame
   d. poor reputation
   e. strong commitment

9. **repatriate**
   a. eat with great vigor
   b. mock in secrecy
   c. name a child after one's parent
   d. return from vacation
   e. return to one's native country

10. **repose**
    a. strange occurrence
    b. rest; relax
    c. state of emergency
    d. bent shape
    e. remote place

11. **reticent**
    a. unjustified
    b. disrespectful
    c. talkative
    d. controversial
    e. reserved

12. **retort**
    a. twist and bend out of shape
    b. return home after a long journey
    c. salvage a useless object
    d. reply in a sharp manner
    e. ignore in the presence of

13. **retroactive**
    a. acknowledging something
    b. caring for history
    c. taking effect from a date in the past
    d. worrying about the past
    e. predicting the future

14. **retrograde**
    a. directed forwards
    b. going nowhere
    c. moving in circles
    d. coming into money
    e. moving backwards

15. **retrospect**
    a. a prediction of the future, a prophecy
    b. a review of a past course of events
    c. a curse by a ghost
    d. a present day occurrence
    e. a survey course

LESSON XVIII: RE-, RETRO-

Exercise D

Solve the crossword puzzle.

Across
6. To identify as already known, to know again. 7. Not revealing one's thoughts or feelings readily. 8. To send (someone) back to his or her own country; to go back to one's fatherland. 10. To say something sharp, angry, or witty in answer to a remark or accusation. 11. To repay. 12. Fame.

Down
1. To restore friendly relations between; to bring into agreement. 2. To lean or lie back in a relaxed manner. 3. A survey or review of a past course of events. 4. To repeat aloud from memory before an audience. 5. Taking effect from a date in the past. 7. To prove to be wrong; to deny. 8. Directed or moving backwards; reverting to an earlier or inferior condition. 9. To rest or sleep.. 11. To say something again for emphasis.

Lesson XIX:
Se-, Super-

SE-
apart, aside, away

*seclude, secure, sedition, seduce, segregation,
supercilious, superfluous, superlative, supersede, supervise*

Word Definitions

seclude
v. to shut (someone) away from other people
"J. D. Salinger refused interview requests and lived a seclude life."
seclusion (n.)
secludere shut off or apart: *se-* apart + *claudere* to shut

secure
v. obtain; fasten or affix to (something); protect against threats
adj. fixed or fastened so as not to give way, become loose, or be lost; protected against attack; free from fear or anxiety
"The Harvard Law grad secured a job as a Supreme Court clerk."
security (n.)
securus safe, untroubled: *se-* apart, away + *cura* care, concern

sedition
n. conduct or speech inciting rebellion against the authority of a state
"Sam Adams' speeches inciting the colonists to rebel against Britain constituted sedition."
seditious (adj.)
seditio sedition: *se-, sed-* apart + *ire* to go

LESSON XIX: SE-, SUPER-

seduce v. to entice (often into sexual activity); to persuade to do something
"He had planned to do social work, but was seduced by Wall Street salaries."
seduction (n.)
seducere lead astray: *se-* away + *ducere* to lead

segregation n. set apart from others; the separation of one group from another
"High school gym classes usually involve segregation of the sexes."
segregate (v.)
segregare to separate from the flock: *se-* apart + *grex, greg-* flock

supercilious adj. having an air of contemptuous superiority
"His disdain and scorn of tradition betrayed a supercilious attitude."
superciliousness (n.)
superciliosus haughty < *supercilium* eyebrow: *super-* above + *cilium* eyelid

superfluous adj. beyond what is needed; extraneous
"Your remarks are superfluous; we've already settled that issue."
superfluousness (n.)
superfluus superfluous: *super-* over + *fluere* to flow

superlative adj. of the highest quality or degree
n. something of the highest degree or excellence
"Her superlative Olympic diving performance earned a score of 10."
super- over + *latus* (past participle of *ferre*, to bring)

supersede v. to take the place of; to supplant
"Today's directive supersedes the previous order on the subject."
supersession (n.)
super- above + *sedere* to sit

supervise v. to oversee and direct the execution of a task or activity
"A foreman supervises the workers and is responsible for quality."
supervision (n.), supervisor (n.)
super- over + *videre* to see

EXERCISE A

Fill in the blanks in the sentences below with the correct form of a word in the scroll above.

1. Venus Williams was once the queen of tennis, but her younger sister Serena has clearly _____ her.

2. Betsey sought out a bench in a _____ clearing where she could be alone with her thoughts.

3. While overt racial _____ is illegal, many African Americans encounter subtle discrimination when they try to buy homes in exclusive neighborhoods.

4. The visitor, _____ by the allure and charms of Venice, decided to stay an extra week.

5. The Secret Service attempted to find a _____ location for the president in case of a terrorist attack.

6. The foreman planned and _____ the project, while the laborers implemented it.

7. Patrick's contemptuous remarks betrayed a _____ attitude that offended the other group members.

8. Most of us would consider an umbrella _____ on a sunny day, but Maria carried one everywhere because her hairstyle could be ruined by rain.

9. Russell Crowe's portrayal of a former tobacco executive torn by feelings of guilt and civic duty in *The Insider* was truly a _____ performance.

10. Patrick Henry's _____ oration inspired patriots to resist British rule.

LESSON XIX: SE-, SUPER-

EXERCISE B

Match the word with the letter of its definition.

1. secluded
2. secure
3. sedition
4. seduce
5. segregation
6. supercilious
7. superfluous
8. superlative
9. supersede
10. supervise

a) conduct inciting rebellion
b) exceed
c) excessive
d) safe
e) act of separating from others
f) hidden or isolated
g) oversee
h) of high quality
i) lead astray
j) haughty; scornful

EXERCISE C

Circle the letter of the definition that best fits the meaning of the bold-faced word.

1. **secluded**
   a. isolated
   b. reserved
   c. exposed
   d. inclusive
   e. tentative

LESSON XIX: SE-, SUPER-

2. **secure**
   a. fortunate
   b. alone
   c. safe
   d. confidential
   e. separate

3. **sedition**
   a. inspiring nationalism
   b. poverty-stricken
   c. appealing to patriotism
   d. inciting rebellion
   e. instilling confidence

4. **seduce**
   a. force into
   b. entice
   c. withdraw from
   d. rebel against
   e. separate

5. **segregation**
   a. leading away from noise
   b. conversing quietly
   c. traveling extensively
   d. separating from others
   e. learning easily

6. **supercilious**
   a. haughty
   b. excessive
   c. unmotivated
   d. unbelievable
   e. silly

7. **superfluous**
   a. unknown
   b. excessive
   c. indifferent
   d. overcome
   e. complex

8. **superlative**
   a. least excessive
   b. best choice
   c. most aloof
   d. greatest quality
   e. smallest part

9. **supersede**
   a. replace
   b. exceed
   c. be ahead
   d. disagree
   e. get ahead

10. **supervise**
    a. conquer
    b. be ahead
    c. overcome
    d. oversee
    e. spend

Exercise D

Solve the crossword puzzle.

Across
2. Unnecessary, especially through being more than enough. 3. To obtain; to affix to or fasten; to protect against threats. 5. Of the highest quality or degree. 6. To entice into (often sexual activity); to persuade to do something inadvisable. 7. To shut (someone) away from other people.

Down
1. Separation of one group from others. 2. To observe and direct the execution of (a task or activity). 3. To take the place of; to supplant. 4. Conduct or speech inciting rebellion against the authority of a state. 5. Having an air of contemptuous superiority.

Lesson XX:
Sub-

SUB-
under, below, up from under

> *subjective, subjugate, sublimate, submarine, submerge, subordinate, suborn, subpoena, subscribe, subservient, substance, substantiate, subterfuge, subvert, succumb, suffocate, suffuse, suggest, suppress, suspend*

Word Definitions

subjective
adj. based on or influenced by personal feeling, tastes, or opinions
"Facts are objective, while opinions are subjective."
subject (n./v.)
subicere to place under: *sub-* under + *iacere* (variant of *jacere*) to throw

subjugate
v. to bring under domination or control, especially by conquest
"Caesar's legions defeated and subjugated the Gauls."
subjugation (n.)
subjugare to bring under the yoke: *sub-* under + *jugare* to marry, to join < *jugum* yoke

sublimate
v. to divert an appetite or urge into a culturally acceptable activity; to go from solid directly to gas or from gas directly to solid
"Some psychologists believe depression is a sublimation of anger."
sublimation (n.)
sublimare to raise, to elevate: *sub-* up from under + *limus* mud, slime

submarine
n. a vessel capable of operating under water
adj. underwater
"Captain Nemo built an ocean-floor base - a submarine home."
sub- under + *marinus* < *mare* sea

LESSON XX: SUB-

submerge　　v. to cause to be under water; to go below the surface
"The physicist <u>submerged</u> an O-ring in a glass of ice water."
submergere to plunge under: *sub-* under + *mergere* to dip, to plunge

subordinate　　adj. lower in rank or position
n. one who is lower in rank or position
v. to place in a lower rank or position
"The exact details are of <u>subordinate</u> concern to the big picture."
subordination (n.)
sub- below + *ordinatus* (past participle of *ordinare* to order, to arrange)

suborn　　v. to bribe or otherwise induce to commit an unlawful act
"The Mafioso who paid the witness to lie was charged with <u>suborning</u> perjury."
subornation (n.)
sub- secretly + *ornare* to equip

subpoena　　v. to summon to court by written order
n. a summons to attend a court
"A <u>subpoena</u> is a document compelling a person to testify."
sub- under + *poena* penalty, punishment

subscribe　　v. to arrange to receive something (such as a periodical); to agree with
"Being a Democrat, I don't <u>subscribe</u> to the Republican economic agenda."
subscription (n.)
subscribere to subscribe, to underwrite: *sub-* under + *scribere* to write

subservient　　adj. subordinate in ability or function; servile
"Conservative Muslims require women to be <u>subservient</u> to men."
subservience (n.)
subservire to serve below or under: *sub-* under + *servire* to serve

substance　　n. a solid basis in fact; a particular kind of matter with uniform properties
"His argument lacked any kind of proof; it had no <u>substance</u>."
substare to hold firm; to stand under: *sub-* under + *stare* to stand; to be

substantiate　　v. to provide evidence to support or prove the truth of; to strengthen
"The experimental evidence <u>substantiated</u> her theory."
substantiation (n.)
substantiare to give substance: *sub-* under + *stantiare* (variant of *stare*, to stand; to be)

subterfuge　　n. a trick or deception used to avoid blame or achieve a goal
"Declaring an offshore bank account in his divorce proceedings was just a <u>subterfuge</u>; he hid most of his assets in a Swiss bank."
subterfugere to evade by stratagem: *subter* beneath, below + *fugere* to flee, to avoid

subvert　　v. to undermine the power and authority of; to corrupt
"He <u>subverted</u> the company president by plotting his ouster."
subversion (n.)
subvertere to overturn or topple: *sub-* from below + *vertere* to turn

LESSON XX: SUB-

succumb   v. to fail to resist (pressure, temptation, etc.); to yield to
"Scores of Panama Canal workers <u>succumbed</u> to yellow fever."
succumbere to surrender, to yield: *sub-* under + *cubare* to lie

suffocate   v. to be unable to breathe; to kill (someone) or die from lack of air
"Putting dirt or sand on a campfire will <u>suffocate</u> the flames."
suffocation (n.)
suffocare to stifle: *sub-* below + *fauces* throat

suffuse   v. to gradually spread through or over
"The smell of roasting turkey <u>suffused</u> the house."
suffusion (n.), suffusive (adj.)
suffundere to pour into: *sub-* into + *fundere* to pour

suggest   v. to put forward for consideration; to hint at
"His muddy boots <u>suggested</u> it was raining outside."
suggestion (n.), suggestive (adj.)
suggerere to suggest, to prompt: *sub-* from below + *gerere* to carry

suppress   v. to end forcibly; to prevent from being expressed or published
"Not wanting to seem rude, the listener <u>suppressed</u> a yawn."
suppression (n.), suppressive (adj.)
supprimere to press down: *sub-* below + *premere* to press, to overwhelm

suspend   v. to halt temporarily; to defer or delay; to hang (something)
"Unpersuaded, he <u>suspended</u> judgment until there were more facts."
suspension (n.)
suspendere to hang up: *sub-* from below + *pendere* to hang

EXERCISE A

Fill in the blanks in the sentences below with the correct form of a word in the scroll above.

1. Her flimsy claim to severe injuries had no _____ in reality.

2. The delicate plants _____ to the cold, snowy weather.

3. Napoleon's army _____ a vast territory before its defeat at the battle of Waterloo.

4. She tried to _____ her laughter, but found his tale so unbelievable she couldn't help giggling.

5. Members of the acting class _____ numerous possibilities for the school musical before agreeing on *Oklahoma!*

LESSON XX: SUB-

6. The court has _____ your testimony; you must appear on Jan. 4 and bring all records of your client's stock trades.

7. His reaction to the painting was purely _____, as he knew nothing about art history and the artist's place in it.

8. To wash clothes by hand, first dissolve the detergent in a bowl and then _____ the dirty laundry to soak in it before scrubbing.

9. Her wild accusations of fraud could not be _____ by investigators.

10. During a trial, it is a crime to _____ perjury.

11. A gardener is _____ to a landscape architect because the latter has more horticultural training.

12. Glass-bottomed boats permit viewing of _____ life.

13. She felt as if she would _____ if she didn't escape from the vile fumes as quickly as possible

14. Police said the thieves used a common _____: two created a distraction by arguing just outside the store, while two others pocketed the jewelry.

15. In the U.S. Army, the rank of lieutenant is _____ to that of a colonel.

16. After a good dinner, fine wine and lively conversation, she calculated he would be so _____ with good will that he would give in to her request.

17. Freud believed that most neurotic behavior springs from unsatisfied primal urges that have been _____.

18. The rebels tried to _____ the dictator's rule by spreading rumors that he had stolen millions of dollars in international aid.

19. Although I read the same newspaper all the time, for variety, each year I _____ to a different magazine.

20. The game was _____ after the third inning due to rain.

EXERCISE B

Match the word with the letter of its definition.

1. **subjective**
2. **subjugate**
3. **sublimate**
4. **submarine**
5. **submerge**
6. **subordinate**
7. **suborn**
8. **subpoena**
9. **subscribe**
10. **subservient**
11. **substance**
12. **substantiate**
13. **subterfuge**
14. **subvert**
15. **succumb**
16. **suffocate**
17. **suffuse**
18. **suggest**
19. **suppress**
20. **suspend**

a) be unable to breath
b) trick or deception used to achieve a goal
c) modify into a culturally acceptable activity
d) forcibly put an end to
e) corrupt
f) servile; lower in ability or function
g) cause to be underwater
h) based on personal feeling, tastes, or opinions
i) fail to resist
j) halt temporarily
k) bring under domination or control
l) vessel capable of operating underwater
m) put forward for consideration
n) provide evidence to prove the truth of
o) summon to attend a court
p) induce to commit an unlawful act
q) lower in rank or position
r) arrange to receive something regularly
s) solid basis in fact
t) gradually spread through or over

EXERCISE C

Circle the letter that best matched the bold-faced word.

1. **subjective**
   a. based on actual facts
   b. based on relations
   c. based on personal feeling, tastes, or opinions
   d. based on people
   e. based on the weather

2. **subjugate**
   a. suspend operations
   b. bring under domination or control
   c. influence
   d. subject to criticism
   e. hide behind or cause to disappear

3. **sublimate**
   a. begin an activity
   b. join a group
   c. divert into an acceptable activity
   d. prove a point
   e. bribe

4. **submarine**
   a. underwater vessel
   b. disabled vehicle
   c. ship
   d. really fast vehicle
   e. airborne vessel

5. **submerge**
   a. allow to be free
   b. bring under control
   c. go under water
   d. modify
   e. trick or deceive

6. **subordinate**
   a. higher in rank
   b. last position
   c. lower in rank
   d. first position
   e. no ranking

7. **suborn**
   a. pass a law
   b. force to testify
   c. hire a lawyer
   d. induce to commit an unlawful act
   e. commit perjury

8. **subpoena**
   a. invitation to attend a party
   b. summons to attend court
   c. gift certificate
   d. legal magazine
   e. deceitful person

9. **subscribe**
   a. bribe someone
   b. order fast food
   c. write a letter
   d. lose something
   e. arrange to receive something

10. **subservient**
    a. commensurate
    b. variant
    c. subordinate
    d dependent
    e. advent

11. **substance**
    a. untruthful
    b. solid basis in fact
    c. sometimes factual
    d. partially true
    e. partially factual

LESSON XX: SUB-

12. **substantiate**
    a. provide testimony at a trial
    b. protect for someone's own good
    c. perpetuate a lie
    d. perform to earn money
    e. provide evidence to prove the truth of

13. **subterfuge**
    a. comic relief
    b. territorial claim
    c. a writ or summons
    d. trick or deception
    e. frugal service

14. **subvert**
    a. condemn
    b. undermine
    c. convey
    d. establish
    e. criticize

15. **succumb**
    a. fail to repeat
    b. deny
    c. fail to resist
    d. succeed
    e. come by easily

16. **suffocate**
    a. choke on food
    b. stop from breathing
    c. gradually decline
    d. able to focus
    e. put forward

17. **suffuse**
    a. gradually spread through
    b. slowly retrain
    c. quickly cover
    d. purposely refuse
    e. willfully conduct

18. **suggest**
    a. offer a fact
    b. prepare for war
    c. perpetuate a crime
    d. put forward for consideration
    e. penetrate after a rain

19. **suppress**
    a. breathe deeply
    b. create a distraction
    c. forcibly put an end to
    d. attain a goal
    e. bribe

20. **suspend**
    a. hang upside down
    b. start quickly
    c. halt temporarily
    d. harm
    e. cancel

Exercise D

Solve the crossword puzzle.

Across
2. Based on or influenced by personal feeling, tastes, or opinions. 3. To bring under domination or control, especially by conquest. 4. To put forward for consideration; hint at. 5. To be unable to breathe; to kill or die from lack of air. 7. To put an end to forcibly; to prevent from being expressed or published. 9. To undermine the power and authority of; to corrupt. 10. To go or put under water. 11. To provide evidence to support or prove the truth of. 13. To summon to court by written order. 14. To fail to resist (pressure, temptation, etc.); yield to.

Down
1. To arrange to receive something (such as a periodical); to agree with. 2. To halt temporarily; to defer or delay. 3. A vessel capable of operating under water. 5. To divert or modify into a culturally acceptable activity; to go from solid directly to gas or from gas directly to solid. 6. A trick or deception used in order to achieve one's goal. 7. Subordinate in ability or function; servile. 8. Lower in rank or position. 9. To bribe or otherwise induce to commit an unlawful act. 12. A solid basis in fact; a particular kind of matter with uniform properties. 13. To gradually spread through or over.

Lesson XXI:
Trans-, Tri-, Ultra-, Uni-, Vice-

TRANS-
across, beyond

TRI-
three

ULTRA-
beyond

UNI-
one

VICE-
in place of

---

transcend, transcribe, transfix, transgress, transitory, translucent, transmute, transparent, transpire, trinity, trisect, triumvirate, ultramarine, ultramundane, unanimous, uniform, unify, unison, unity, viceroy

---

Word Definitions

transcend
v. to be or go beyond the range or limits of; to surpass
"Unexplainable miracles <u>transcend</u> our limited understanding."
trans- across + *scandere* to climb

transcribe
v. to put into written or printed form
"The secretary <u>transcribed</u> Trump's speech and gave copies to the media."
transcription (n.)
transcribere to copy: *trans-* across + *scribere* to write

transfix
v. to make motionless with horror, wonder, or astonishment; to pierce with a sharp implement or weapon
"She was <u>transfixed</u> by his malevolent stare and twisted smile."
transfixion (n.)
transfigere to pierce through: *trans-* across + *figere* to pierce, to fasten

LESSON XXI: TRANS-, TRI-, ULTRA-, UNI-, VICE-

transgress	**v.** to go beyond the limits set (by a moral, principle, standard, etc.); to exceed or overstep "To commit a crime is, by definition, to transgress the law." *transgression (n.)* *transgredi* to step across: *trans-* across + *gradi* to step, to walk
transitory	**adj.** fleeting; short-lived; temporary "An eclipse is a transitory phenomenon." *transitoriness (n.)* *transire* to go over; to go across: *trans-* over, across + *ire* to go
translucent	**adj.** allowing some light to pass through; semi-transparent "Stained glass is translucent, while clear glass is transparent." *translucence (n.)* *translucere*: to shine through: *trans-* across (through) + *lucere* to shine
transmute	**v.** to change in form, nature, or substance; to transform "Alchemists attempted in vain to transmute base metals into gold." *transmutation (n.)* *transmutare* to change about: *trans-* over + *mutare* to change
transparent	**adj.** (of a substance) allowing light to pass through so that objects behind can be distinctly seen; (of someone) easy to see through "His true motives were transparent to everyone but his adoring wife." *transparency (n.)* *transparere* to show through: *trans-* across (through) + *parere* to show
transpire	**v.** to become known or leak out; to happen "What transpired between them so that they became enemies?" *transpiration (n.)* *trans-* across + *spirare* to breathe, to exhale
trinity	**n.** a triad of related things, ideas or people; the Holy Trinity (the three forms of God in Christianity: father, son, and holy spirit) "The trinity of Germany, Italy, and Japan formed WWII's Axis." *trinitas* three or the Holy Trinity < *trinus* triple or a set of three
trisect	**v.** to divide into three equal parts "With the pizza trisected, the three friends received equal portions." *trisection (n.)* *tri-* three + *secare* to divide, to cut
triumvirate	**n.** a group of three powerful or notable people or things "The triumvirate of Octavian, Anthony, and Lepidus shared power." *triumviri* board of three < *tri-* three
ultramarine	**n.** a blue pigment made from powdered lapis lazuli; a vivid or purplish blue; of or from a place beyond the sea "Ultramarine enamels gave Egyptian coffins a deep blue cast." *ultra-* beyond + *marinus* of the sea < *mare* sea

LESSON XXI: TRANS-, TRI-, ULTRA-, UNI-, VICE-

ultramundane adj. existing outside the known world or universe; outside the orbit of the Earth and other planets
"The ultramundane is all the lies beyond the known world."
ultra- beyond + *mundanus* worldly < *mundus, mundi* world

unanimous adj. fully in agreement; universally in accord
"The court's decision was unanimous, surprising those who had expected Justice Scalia to dissent."
unanimity (n.)
unanimus acting in accord: *uni-* one, single + *animus* mind

uniform adj. the same in all cases and at all times; unvarying
n. required clothing for a particular group
"They all agreed, so they were of uniform opinion."
uniformity (n.)
uniformis having only one shape: *uni-* one + *forma* shape

unify v. to make into or become a unit; to consolidate
"Covalent bonds unify one hydrogen and two oxygen atoms to make water."
unifier (n.)
unificare to unite: *uni-* one + *facere* to make

unison n. simultaneous (of an action or utterance); of one accord
"The crowd rose in unison when the 'Hallelujah Chorus' began."
unisonus in unison: *uni-* one + *sonus* sound

unity n. the state of being united; forming a complex whole
"'Unity' is mathematicians' formal term for the number one."
unitas oneness < *unus* one

viceroy n. a ruler exercising authority on behalf of a sovereign
"Robert Clive became governor - or viceroy - of colonial India."
viceroyship, viceroyalty (n.)
vice in place of + *rex, regis* king

EXERCISE A

Fill in the blanks in the sentences below with the correct form of a word in the scroll above.

1. If you _____ an object, you will get three equal parts.

2. During the horror movie, her eyes were _____ on the screen.

3. The _____ was accountable to the king, and the king alone.

4. Like clockwork each spring, wriggly tadpoles _____ into tiny frogs.

LESSON XXI: TRANS-, TRI-, ULTRA-, UNI-, VICE-

5. The official result was _____; the entire class voted to go on a field trip at the end of the year.

6. Sean Penn's superb portrayal of a retarded man in *I Am Sam* _____ all his previous efforts.

7. Inconsistent nutrition, water, and light do not produce _____ results in plants' growth.

8. The new _____ curtains made the room appear lighter and brighter.

9. He could _____ the country in support of universal health care if he used the bully pulpit to promote it.

10. The artist's favorite color, _____, reminded him of the magnificent ocean views from his villa.

11. As soon as class was over, the student took time to _____ the pertinent information from his recording of the lecture.

12. Drinking, smoking, and cursing were a _____ of evils in the eyes of the moralist.

13. There may exist _____forms of life in dimensions beyond our solar system, but we humans are fundamentally incapable of comprehending them.

14. His flash of anger was _____; soon he was in good spirits.

15. The _____and cohesion of our team demonstrated on the field led us to victory.

16. The disciplinarian was appalled by the mischief that _____ in his absence.

17. The school chorus sang in _____ for the boldest and most dramatic effect.

18. Every Friday, the rabbi warned his congregation not to _____ against God's commandments for his chosen people.

19. A _____ of the world's three economic powers convened annually in Geneva.

20. Glass greenhouses remain _____for decades, while clear plastics, although more durable, can become scratched and cloudy quickly.

LESSON XXI: TRANS-, TRI-, ULTRA-, UNI-, VICE-

EXERCISE B

Match the word with the letter of its definition.

1. transcend
2. transcribe
3. transfix
4. transgress
5. transitory
6. translucent
7. transmute
8. transparent
9. transpire
10. trinity
11. trisect
12. triumvirate
13. ultramarine
14. ultramundane
15. unanimous
16. uniform
17. unify
18. unison
19. unity
20. viceroy

a) a group of three powerful people or things
b) make motionless
c) ruler exercising authority on behalf of a sovereign
d) divide into three equal parts
e) existing outside the known world
f) to make into or become a unit
g) of one accord
h) three closely related things or ideas
i) to change in form, nature, or substance
j) short-lived
k) to be or go beyond the range or limits of
l) the same in all cases; unvarying
m) a complex whole
n) allowing light to pass through partially
o) to put (music or speech) in written or printed form
p) easily seen through
q) to go beyond set limits
r) fully in agreement
s) to become known or leak out
t) a blue pigment made from powdered lapis lazuli

EXERCISE C

Circle the letter of the definition which best fits the meaning of the bold-faced word.

1. **transcend**
   a. go around
   b. lag behind
   c. surpass
   d. unite
   e. act on another's behalf

2. **transcribe**
   a. write a story
   b. put into written or printed form
   c. create
   d. sing a song
   e. translate

3. **transfix**
   a. mend something broken
   b. pass out by holding your breath
   c. support something heavy
   d. make motionless with horror, wonder, or astonishment
   e. scream in fear

4. **transgress**
   a. exceed or overstep
   b. cross a river
   c. pardon for sins
   d. carry off
   e. make amends

169

LESSON XXI: TRANS-, TRI-, ULTRA-, UNI-, VICE-

5. **transitory**
   a. able to take a direct object
   b. short-lived
   c. unchanging
   d. in limbo
   e. taking from one place to another

6. **translucent**
   a. opaque
   b. semi-transparent
   c. muddy
   d. clear
   e. shiny, bright

7. **transmute**
   a. make mute
   b. hold back
   c. be unable to talk
   d. transform
   e. turn upside down

8. **transparent**
   a. difficult to understand
   b. clear or obvious
   c. smooth
   d. unclear
   e. translucent

9. **transpire**
   a. become known
   b. shrink away
   c. come around
   d. see in the future
   e. predict

10. **trinity**
    a. two closely related things
    b. unrelated matters
    c. three closely related things
    d. multiple related things
    e. three unrelated things

11. **trisect**
    a. execute
    b. divide into three equal parts
    c. combine three equal parts
    d. divide into parts
    e. project

12. **triumvirate**
    a. small group of powerful men
    b. large group of things
    c. group of two things
    d. group of three powerful people or things
    e. individualist

13. **ultramarine**
    a. marine clay
    b. gemstone
    c. blue pigment
    d. artist's brush
    e. mollusk

14. **ultramundane**
    a. just coming into existence
    b. existing everywhere
    c. extra special
    d. existing outside the known world
    e. near an exit

15. **unanimous**
    a. fully in agreement
    b. suffering conflict
    c. disagreement
    d. peaceful
    e. fully hidden

16. **uniform**
    a. sometimes varying
    b. always the same
    c. sometimes the same
    d. always different
    e. inconsistent

17. **unify**
    a. divide
    b. judge
    c. consolidate
    d. control
    e. care for

LESSON XXI: TRANS-, TRI-, ULTRA-, UNI-, VICE-

18. unison
   a. simultaneous (of an action)
   b. hard of hearing
   c. dissonance
   d. calmness
   e. brotherly love

19. unity
   a. forming a government
   b. walking together
   c. looking under
   d. oneness
   e. creating a puzzle

20. viceroy
   a. king
   b. sovereign's authority
   c. monarchy
   d. queen
   e. ruler exercising authority on behalf of a sovereign

Exercise D

Across
1. The state of being united, forming a complex whole. 5. Allowing light to pass through partially; semi-transparent. 7. To change in form, nature, or substance; to transform. 12. Fully in agreement; universally in accord. 15. To go beyond the limits set by (a moral, principle, standard, etc.); to exceed or overstep. 16. A group consisting of three closely related people, things or ideas. 17. Simultaneous action or utterance. 18. To put into written or printed form.

Down
2. Fleeting; temporary. 3. A group of three powerful or notable people or things. 4. A ruler exercising authority on behalf of a sovereign. 6. Allowing light to pass through so that objects behind can be distinctly seen. 7. To divide into three equal parts. 8. To make known; to happen. 9. To make into or become a unit; to consolidate. 10. To be or go beyond the range or limits of; to surpass. 11. To make motionless with horror, wonder, or astonishment; to pierce. 12. The same in all cases and at all times. 13. A blue pigment made from powdered lapis lazuli; of or from a place beyond the sea. 14. Existing outside the known world or the universe.

Test 4

Choose the correct meaning for the underlined vocabulary word in each sentence.

1. "I wished, as it were, to procrastinate all that related to my feelings of affection until the great object, which swallowed up every habit of my nature, should be completed."

   Frankenstein by Mary Shelley

   (a) postpone   (b) justify   (c) benefit   (d) comprehend   (e) obtain

2. "For Tahiti is smiling and friendly; it is like a lovely woman graciously prodigal of her charm and beauty; and nothing can be more conciliatory than the entrance into the harbour."

   Moon and Sixpence by Somerset Maugham

   (a) frugal   (b) caring   (c) extravagant   (d) colorful   (e) skilled

3. "Initiate me into all those mysteries which profane eyes never beheld."

   The History of Tom Jones by Henry Fielding

   (a) tardy   (b) secular   (c) useless   (d) religious   (e) careless

4. "People noticed his propensity for walking in rough weather, and watched him curiously as he did his rounds."

   Alexander's Bridge by Willa Cather

   (a) extension   (b) skill   (c) speed   (d) tendency   (e) opportunity

5. "For an instant the wrinkles were smoothed away, the nose drew away from the chin, the lower lip ceased to protrude and the mouth to mumble, the dull eyes regained their fire, the drooping figure expanded."

   Memoirs of Sherlock Holmes by Sir Arthur Conan Doyle

   (a) excel   (b) withdraw   (c) excite   (d) annoy   (e) bulge

6. "When parties in a state are violent, he offered a wonderful contrivance to reconcile them."

Gulliver's Travels by Jonathan Swift

(a) explain to   (b) bring into between   (c) argue with   (d) disapprove of   (e) judge

7. "My opinion is confirmed, and I reiterate my advice."

A Tale Of Two Cities by Charles Dickens

(a) think about   (b) exercise   (c) repeat   (d) rest   (e) reserve

8. "She had told him she was not now at Marlott, but had been curiously reticent as to her actual address, and the only course was to go to Marlott and inquire for it."

Tess of the d'Urbervilles by Thomas Hardy

(a) silent   (b) unjustified   (c) talkative   (d) controversial   (e) disrespectful

9. "But suppose that he were to retort, 'Thrasymachus, what do you mean?"

The Republic by Plato

(a) ignore completely   (b) say again   (c) reply sharply   (d) twist the words   (e) whisper

10. "The neighborhood extracted considerable eager conversation from it; argument, rebuttal, suspicion, certainty, retrospect, and prophecy."

RebeccaOfSunnybrookFarm by Kate Douglas Wiggin

(a) survey   (b) predict   (c) prevent   (d) review   (e) curse

11. "Guards, musketeers, officers, soldiers, murmurs, uneasiness, dispersed, vanished, died away; there was an end of menace and sedition."

The Man in the Iron Mask by Alexandre Dumas

(a) poverty   (b) rebellion   (c) patriotism   (d) exposure   (e) separation

12. "As the dancers poured out of the hall, Frome, drawing back behind the projecting storm-door, watched the segregation of the grotesquely muffled groups, in which a moving lantern ray now and then lit up a face flushed with food and dancing."

Ethan Frome by Edith Wharton

(a) withdrawing   (b) killing   (c) conversing   (d) separation   (e) traveling

TEST 4

13. "Her face beamed with satisfaction when the guest eyed the appointments with a supercilious glance."

    The Lair of the White Worm by Bram Stoker

    (a) Haughty (b) silly (c) excessive (d) believable (e) knowing

14. "But as time went on he led a more and more austere life, refusing everything superfluous, and finally he accepted nothing but rye-bread once a week."

    Father Sergius by Leo Tolstoy

    (a) unknown (b) indifferent (c) unnecessary (d) unbelievable (e) unmotivated

15. "When those who have the deliberative power elect each other, and the son succeeds to the father, and when they can supersede the laws, such a government is of necessity a strict oligarchy."

    A Treatise on Government by Aristotle

    (a) exceed (b) replace (c) break (d) disagree with (e) overcome

16. "Communism deprives no man of the power to appropriate the products of society; all that it does is to deprive him of the power to subjugate the labour of others by means of such appropriation."

    The Communist Manifesto by Karl Marx & Frederic Engles

    (a) suspend (b) influence (c) prove (d) bribe (e) control

17. "Jezebel went forth and forged letters to the nobles and wise men, in the King's name, and ordered them to proclaim a fast and set Naboth on high before the people, and suborn two witnesses to swear that he had blasphemed."

    The Innocents Abroad by Mark Twain

    (a) force (b) bribe (c) command (d) summon (e) subpoena

18. "Mabbott does not substantiate this claim, but it is surely not unreasonable."

    The Angel of the Odd by Edgar Allan Poe

    (a) perpetuate (b) condemn (c) fail (d) prove (e) corrupt

19. "Now when Morning, clad in her robe of saffron, had begun to suffuse light over the earth, Jove called the gods in council on the topmost crest of serrated Olympus."

    The Iliad by Homer

    (a) refrain (b) refuse (c) spread (d) conduct (e) conduct

20. "He maintained that it was absolutely impossible to impress upon any body whatever a velocity of 12,000 yards per second; that even with such a velocity a projectile of such a weight could not transcend the limits of the earth's atmosphere."

From The Earth To The Moon by Jules Verne

(a) surpass (b) unite (c) create (d) cover (e) end

21. "You transmute the commonest traits into gold of your own; but after all there are no new names."

The Arrow of Gold by Joseph Conrad

(a) talk (b) see through (c) transform (d) opaque (e) clear

22. "All memorable events, I should say, transpire in morning time and in a morning atmosphere."

Walden by Henry David Thoreau

(a) predict (b) understand (c) evaporate (d) happen (e) live

23. "Most of the American genealogists commence their traditions like the stories for children, with three brothers, taking especial care that one of the triumvirate shall be the progenitor of any of the same name...."

The Pioneers by James Fenimore Cooper

(a) individual (b) twosome (c) threesome (d) foursome (e) many

24. "We are all unanimous in that wish, I suppose," said Elinor, "in spite of the insufficiency of wealth."

Sense and Sensibility by Jane Austen

(a) suffering in conflict (b) in agreement (c) always different
(d) coming into existence (e) seeing the future

25. "When the chief has finished his prayer or exhortation, he says, 'I have done,' upon which there is a general exclamation in unison."

The Adventures of Captain Bonneville by Washington Irving

(a) unusually calm (b) walking together (c) ruling authority (d) brotherly love
(e) in one voice

Appendix A

Quizzes

QUIZ 1: CHAPTERS 1-5

Quiz 1
for Chapters 1-5

1. "The rank, wealth, and eminent character of the deceased must have insured the strictest scrutiny into every _____ circumstance." *House of Seven Gables* by Nathaniel Hawthorne.

2. "Davis had declared limes a _____ article, and solemnly vowed to publicly ferrule the first person who was found breaking the law." *Little Women* by Louisa May Alcott

3. "You, my creator, _____ me; what hope can I gather from your fellow creatures, who owe me nothing?" *Frankenstein* by Mary Shelley

4. "The only member of our small society who positively refused to _____ himself to circumstances, was Jip." *David Copperfield* by Charles Dickens

5. "The boy's soul was steeped in melancholy; his feelings were in happy _____ with his surroundings." *Tom Sawyer* by Mark Twain

6. "The day seemed, by _____ with my recent confinement, dazzlingly bright, the sky a glowing blue." *The War Of The Worlds* by H.G. Wells

7. "He went therefore to his appointment with Athos without a second, determines to be satisfied with those his _____ should choose." *The Three Musketeers* by Alexandra Dumas

8. "The priest and the negro knelt and murmured together the evening _____ and a prayer for the dead." *The Awakening and Selected Short Stories* by Kate Chopin

9. "The eagle took flight, and pouncing upon a hare, brought it at once as an offering to his _____." *Fables* by Aesop

10. "SOCRATES: And does not this line, reaching from corner to corner, _____ each of these spaces?" *Meno* by Plato

QUIZ 2: CHAPTERS 6-10

Quiz 2 for Chapters 6-10

1. "Hence, the spare boats, spare spars, and spare lines and harpoons, and spare everything almost, but a spare captain and _____ ship?" *Moby Dick* by Herman Melville

2. "With an enemy on each side of him, he slipped swiftly out of the way and let them _____ and kill each other." *The Innocence of Father Brown* by Gilbert K. Chesterton

3. "As to the 52-foot linear raters, praised so much by the writer, I am warmed up by his approval of their performances; but, as far as any clear conception goes, the descriptive phrase, so precise to the comprehension of a yachtsman, _____ no definite image in my mind." *The Mirror of the Sea* by Joseph Conrad

4. "Almost daily he whetted his keen knife and scraped and whittled at his young beard to _____ this degrading emblem of apehood." *Tarzan of the Apes* by Edgar Rice Burroughs

5. "Scarcely were we clear when the foremast dropped down on the fastenings, dashing the jib-boom into the water with its load of _____ human beings." *Dead Men Tell No Tales* by E.W. Hornung

6. "Afterwards, the wall was whitewashed or scraped down, I know not which, and the _____ disappeared." *Notre-Dame Paris* by Victor Hugo

7. "He gave her the Indian _____ for firebug, or fire-fly." *A Horse's Tale* by Mark Twain

8. "Nothing was found to _____ him in any way, and there the matter dropped." *Memoirs of Sherlock Holmes* by Sir Arthur Conan Doyle

9. "Nay, but they are not to take in a decoction or in nauseous form, so you need not snub that so charming nose, or I shall point out to my friend Arthur what woes he may have to endure in seeing so much beauty that he so loves so much _____ ." *Dracula* by Bram Stroker

10. "And beneath that roof was an aerial ooze of vegetation, a monstrous, parasitic dripping of _____ life-forms that rooted in death and lived on death." *The Red One* by Jack London

Quiz 3 for Chapters 11-15

1. "This one is built against the solid rock, and it would take ten experienced miners, duly furnished with the requisite tools, as many years to _____ it." *The Count of Monte Cristo* by Alexandre Dumas

2. "The Prince was waiting for an opportunity to _____ ." *The Yellow Crayon* by E. Phillip Oppenheim

3. "It would almost seem as if Nature herself had tried to _____ the evil sign and sounds of active life." *The Lair of the White Worm* by Bram Stoker

4. "It was considered hardly _____ enough to be allowed to keep its place in the council chamber of Massachusetts." *Grandfather's Chair* by Nathaniel Hawthorne

5. "Now I am twenty-eight and am in reality more _____ than many schoolboys of fifteen." *Frankenstein* by Mary Shelley

6. "It was a mere falsification of the law of aerial _____ but it startled, almost terrified me." *Can Such Things Be?* By Ambrose Bierce

7. "He tried not to pay any attention to a strange rustling sound that he heard, as of an unseen _____ drawing near to listen to his words." *The Emerald City of Oz* by L. Frank Baum

8. "And I quickly learned to be afraid of him and his _____ pranks." *Before Adam* by Jack London

9. "Images, visions, _____ with particular force, men withdrawn from the sights and sounds of active live." *Chance* by Joseph Conrad

10. "Then silent, scarcely uttering an _____ of admiration, they gazed, they gazed, they contemplated." *Round the Moon* by Jules Verne

Quiz 4 for Chapters 16–21

1. "There in the flickering light of the lamp was the machine sure enough, squat, ugly and askew; a thing of brass, ebony, ivory, and _____ glimmering quartz." *The Time Machine* by H.G. Wells

2. "There we have command and power in their _____ form." *War and Peace* by Leo Tolstoy

3. "I will therefore go upstairs and _____ upon that couch which I have never ceased to flood with my tears from the day Ulysses set out for the city with a hateful name." *The Odyssey* by Homer

4. "She often tried to _____ Darcy into disliking her guest, by talking of their supposed marriage, and planning his happiness in such an alliance." *Pride and Prejudice* by Jane Austen

5. "Only in _____ can I mark the almost imperceptible growth of my desire." *John Barleycorn* by Jack London

6. "Do you _____ to Middlemarch library?" *Middlemarch* by George Eliot

7. "I know what your object is, as I _____ you do mine." *Tom Swift In The Land of Wonders* by Victor Appleton

8. "Why not still _____ over the untamed yet obedient element?" *Frankenstein* by Mary Shelley

9. "I was asked to _____ my visit, as a favor to herself, because she had her own reasons for wishing it." *I Say No* by Wilkie Collins

10. "I don't know how long she would have gone on "conversing" and incidentally, helping to _____ the beautifully stocked linen closets of that well-to-do German household." *Chance* by James Conrad

Answer Key

Lesson I

A. 1. abscess. 2. abdicated. 3. abduct. 4. abject. 5. abjure. 6. abominate or abhor. 7. abstained. 8. abstemious. 9. abstruse. 10. abused. 11. averse. 12. averted. 13. avocation. 14. abrogate. 15. abrupt. 16. absconded. 17. absolved. 18. absorb. 19. abhor or abominate. 20. abrasion.
B. 1. n. 2. e. 3. k or q. 4. s. 5. o. 6. q or k. 7. j. 8. p. 9. r. 10. g. 11. f. 12. c. 13. h. 14. t. 15. m. 16. b. 17. l. 18. i. 19. a. 20. d.
C. 1. b. 2. a. 3. c. 4. a. 5. b. 6. b. 7. b. 8. a. 9. b. 10. c. 11. a. 12. c. 13. a. 14. c. 15. b. 16. b. 17. a. 18. c. 19. b. 20. a.

Lesson II

A. 1. adopt. 2. arraignment. 3. appear. 4. assumption. 5. accord. 6. admonished. 7. adaptable. 8. adequate. 9. assimilate. 10. affliction. 11. ad hoc. 12. adversary. 13. advent. 14. aggregation. 15. appease. 16. annexation. 17. adhered. 18. adjoined. 19. adverse. 20. adjacent.
B. 1. d. 2. o. 3. p. 4. l. 5. j. 6. m. 7. k. 8. c. 9. s. 10. g. 11. a. 12. f. 13. r. 14. t. 15. b. 16. e. 17. h. 18. n. 19. i. 20. q.
C. 1. b. 2. a. 3. b. 4. c. 5. a. 6. b. 7. c. 8. e. 9. e. 10. a. 11. c. 12. a. 13. c. 14. a. 15. b. 16. c. 17. e. 18. b. 19. e. 20. c.

Lesson III

A. 1. ambiguous. 2. anterior. 3. antedate. 4. antebellum. 5. ambivalent. 6. antediluvian. 7. ambidextrous. 8. ante meridian. 9. antecedent. 10. anticipate.
B. 1. i. 2. d. 3. g. 4. h. 5. a. 6. j. 7. c. 8. b. 9. e. 10. f.
C. 1. b. 2. c. 3. b. 4. a. 5. b. 6. c. 7. e. 8. d. 9. a. 10. c.

Lesson IV

A. 1. biceps. 2. benevolence. 3. bicameral. 4. bicuspid. 5. benediction. 6. bifurcate. 7. bonus. 8. beneficent. 9. bona fide. 10. bipartisan. 11. bisected. 12. bilateral. 13. benign. 14. benefactors. 15. bilingual.
B. 1. f. 2. b. 3. g. 4. m. 5. i. 6. a. 7. c. 8. h. 9. o. 10. j. 11. k. 12. e. 13. l. 14. d. 15. n.
C. 1. d. 2. d. 3. a. 4. a. 5. d. 6. e. 7. b. 8. a. 9. e. 10. a. 11. d. 12. d. 13. a. 14. e. 15. b.

Lesson V

A. 1. circumference. 2. controversy. 3. circumlocution. 4. circuitous. 5. contravened. 6. circumnavigate. 7. circumvent. 8. contrast. 9. circumspect. 10. contraceptives. 11. contraband. 12. circumscribed. 13. contradicting. 14. circulated. 15. circumstantial.
B. 1. k. 2. n. 3. b. 4. h. 5. l. 6. g. 7. d. 8. m. 9. a. 10. i. 11. o. 12. c. 13. e. 14. j. 15. f.
C. 1. a. 2. d. 3. e. 4. b. 5. e. 6. c. 7. a. 8. c. 9. d. 10. b. 11. e. 12. c. 13. c. 14. a. 15. d.

ANSWER KEY

Lesson VI

A. 1. coherent. 2. conference. 3. correspondent. 4. contrite. 5. convened. 6. collateral. 7. congenital. 8. commerce. 9. concoct. 10. coalesce. 11. consecrated. 12. condone. 13. concord. 14. compositions. 15. collision. 16. commiserated. 17. commission. 18. collaborated. 19. collusion. 20. corroborated.

B. 1. j. 2. m. 3. h. 4. p. 5. q. 6. g. 7. e. 8. l. 9. r. 10. b. 11. a. 12. o. 13. c. 14. i. 15. n. 16. f. 17. k. 18. t. 19. s. 20. d.

C. 1. e. 2. a. 3. b. 4. d. 5. a. 6. b. 7. c. 8. d. 9. b. 10. b. 11. d. 12. e. 13. b. 14. d. 15. b. 16. e. 17. c. 18. d. 19. a. 20. d.

Test 1

1. abjure — a. forswear
2. abominate — b. detest
3. abrasion — d. scrape
4. abstemious — d. eating and drinking in moderation
5. abstruse — a. complex
6. averse — b. strongly disinclined
7. accord — b. agreement
8. admonish — c. reprimand
9. annex — a. attachment
10. assimilates — e. incorporates
11. ambiguous — b. unclear
12. anterior — a. preexisting
13. benign — b. harmless
14. bifurcates — c. divides into two
15. bona fide — c. authentic
16. circuitous — b. indirect
17. circumspect — c. prudent
18. contradict — e. say the opposite of
19. contravene — e. violate
20. coalesced — b. bound together
21. collateral — a. coinciding
22. collusion — c. secret agreement
23. condoned — e. forgave
24. congenital — c. present at birth
25. corroborate — d. support

Lesson VII

A. 1. demolish. 2. devoured. 3. demented. 4. demoted. 5. deciduous. 6. depreciate. 7. debase. 8. deter. 9. devious. 10. despise. 11. deviated. 12. describe. 13. descendant. 14. desiccate. 15. dependent. 16. decadence. 17. despondent. 18. depend. 19. deflation. 20. dedicated.

B. 1. t. 2. m. 3. k. 4. n. 5. o. 6. e. 7. l. 8. c. 9. s. 10. b. 11. j. 12. g. 13. q. 14. h. 15. p. 16. i. 17. a. 18. r. 19. d. 20. f.

C. 1. d. 2. a. 3. c. 4. d. 5. b. 6. d. 7. b. 8. a. 9. c. 10. b. 11. d. 12. b. 13. a. 14. c. 15. d. 16. c. 17. a. 18. b. 19. a. 20. c.

ANSWER KEY

Lesson VIII

A. 1. dilapidated. 2. dispel. 3. diffident. 4. discord. 5. dual. 6. disintegrated. 7. distract. 8. duplicate. 9. discredit. 10. distortion. 11. duet. 12. dissent. 13. dissident. 14. duplicity. 15. diverge. 16. discern. 17. duplex. 18. discrepancy. 19. discontent. 20 duo.
B. 1. e. 2. m. 3. j. 4. i. 5. k. 6. n. 7. o. 8. l. 9. h. 10. d. 11. a. 12. c. 13. p. 14. s. 15. b. 16. t. 17. g. 18. r. 19. f. 20. q.
C. 1. d. 2. c. 3. b. 4. e. 5. d. 6. b. 7. d. 8. d. 9. b. 10. d. 11. e. 12. c. 13. e. 14. e. 15. b. 16. d. 17. c. 18. e. 19. a. 20. c.

Lesson IX

A. 1. extravagant. 2. exhilarated. 3. exorbitant. 4. eminent. 5. equilateral. 6. eradicated. 7. excise. 8. exonerate. 9. equities. 10. elaborate. 11. extroverts. 12. extraneous. 13. equivalent. 14. enervated. 15. extracurricular. 16. emigrated. 17. erosion. 18. equilibrium. 19. evoke. 20. exclusive.
B. 1. g. 2. o. 3. i. 4. m. 5. t. 6. f. 7. s. 8. e. 9. b. 10. d. 11. k. 12. n. 13. h. 14. p. 15. j. 16. a. 17. l. 18. q. 19. c. 20. r.
C. 1. d. 2. e. 3. a. 4. b. 5. c. 6. b. 7. d. 8. b. 9. c. 10. d. 11. a. 12. a. 13. a. 14. e. 15. b. 16. a. 17. a. 18. e. 19. b. 20. e .

Lesson X

A. 1. invite. 2. induct. 3. impelled. 4. indorsed. 5. irradiation. 6. invocation . 7. intend. 8. imminent. 9. incise. 10. illuminate. 11. incarceration. 12. impression. 13. imbibe. 14. inscribe. 15. implicating. 16. inclusive. 17. immigrate . 18. impugns . 19. illustrations . 20. insurgents.
B. 1. h. 2. b. 3. l. 4. t. 5. k. 6. q. 7. d. 8. a. 9. f. 10. j. 11. s. 12. m. 13. g. 14. c. 15. r. 16. i. 17. n. 18. e. 19. p. 20. o.
C. 1. e. 2 c. 3. b. 4. a. 5. c. 6. b. 7. d. 8. a. 9. e. 10. b. 11. b. 12. c. 13. d. 14. e. 15. c. 16. d. 17. b. 18. a. 19. c. 20. c.

Lesson XI

A. 1. impeccable. 2. inordinate. 3. irreverent. 4. implacable. 5. immature. 6. illegible. 7. insubordinate. 8. irrevocable. 9. impunity. 10. inefficient. 11. ingratitude. 12. immaculate. 13. inhospitable. 14. irrelevant. 15. inflexible. 16. inaccessible. 17. illiterate. 18. incessant. 19. irregular. 20. insoluble.
B. 1. g. 2. n. 3. r. 4. a. 5. i. 6. h. 7. p. 8. t. 9. m. 10. d. 11. b. 12. s. 13. o. 14. c. 15. k. 16. f. 17. e. 18. q. 19. j. 20. l.
C. 1. d. 2. b. 3. a. 4. b. 5. b. 6. c. 7. e. 8. d. 9. a. 10. e. 11. e. 12. b. 13. a. 14. c. 15. b. 16. b. 17. b. 18. d. 19. b. 20. d.

ANSWER KEY

Test 2

1. decadence — a. moral or physical decline
2. deciduous — c. shedding annually
3. demented — b. insane
4. descendant — d. offspring
5. despondent — b. hopeless
6. deviate — e. depart
7. diffident — a. lacking self-confidence
8. discord — c. lack of agreement or harmony
9. dispel — b. scatter or make disappear
10. distort — e. misrepresent
11. dual — b. double
12. duplicity — d. deception
13. emigrate — a. migrate
14. enervates — e. weakens
15. excise — d. tax
16. equilibrium — b. balance
17. extraneous — c. irrelevant
18. impel — e. motivate
19. insurgents — b. rebels
20. invocation — c. appeal
21. implacable — b. unrelenting
22. incessant — a. continuous
23. insoluble — c. hopeless
24. irrelevant — d. extraneous
25. irreverent — b. disrespectful

Lesson XII

A. 1. introduce. 2. introspection. 3. interpret. 4. interjection. 5. intersect. 6. intercede. 7. intramural. 8. interlude. 9. interest. 10. interstices. 11. interregnum. 12. intermediary. 13. intermittent. 14. Intravenous. 15. introvert. 16. interpolate. 17. internecine. 18. intervene. 19. intermission. 20 international.
B. 1. h. 2. o. 3. d. 4. a. 5. e. 6. k. 7. i. 8. l. 9. g. 10. b. 11. j. 12. s. 13. c. 14. f. 15. q. 16. n. 17. p. 18. r. 19. m. 20. t.
C. 1. c. 2. a. 3. e. 4. d. 5. a. 6. b. 7. a. 8. a. 9. c. 10. e. 11. b. 12. e. 13. b. 14. c. 15. b. 16. d.

Lesson XIII

A. 1. magnificent . 2. malign. 3. magnanimous. 4. multifarious. 5. malady. 6. major. 7. malefactor. 8. malevolent or malicious. 9. multilateral. 10. magnitude. 11. malicious or malevolent. 12. malediction. 13. maladjusted. 14. magnate. 15. majority. 16. malnutrition. 17. malignant. 18. multitude. 19. malodorous. 20. malpractice.
B. 1. k. 2. n. 3. p. 4. s. 5. c. 6. l. 7. m. 8. o. 9. b. 10. q. 11. g. 12. t. 13. d. 14. f. 15. h. 16. r. 17. j. 18. e. 19. i. 20. a .
C. 1. c. 2. d. 3. b. 4. a. 5. a. 6. e. 7. c. 8. d. 9. b. 10. d. 11. a. 12. c. 13. e. 14. c. 15. a. 16. d. 17. e. 18. a. 19. d. 20. c.

ANSWER KEY

Lesson XIV

A. 1. obviate. 2. obsessing. 3. omniscient. 4. obliterate. 5. obtruding. 6. omnipotent. 7. obsequious. 8. obnoxious. 9. obstacles. 10. obfuscated. 11. obdurate or obstinate. 12. obligation. 13. omnipresent. 14. obstinate or obdurate. 15. omnivorous.
B. 1. g. 2. b. 3. d. 4. h. 5. a. 6. m. 7. f. 8. l. 9. i. 10. k. 11. n. 12. c. 13. j. 14. e. 15. o.
C. 1. d. 2. a. 3. b. 4. e. 5. c. 6. c. 7. a. 8. b. 9. d. 10. d. 11. a. 12. c. 13. d. 14. c. 15. b.

Lesson XV

A. 1. permeable. 2. pernicious. 3. persevere. 4. Percolates 5. perspicacious. 6. perpetuated. 7. perturbed. 8. perforated . 9. pertinent. 10. perplexed. 11. permutations. 12. perspire. 13. perspective. 14. perfection. 15. permission.
B. 1. a. 2. n. 3. j. 4. c. 5. o. 6. f. 7. b. 8. m. 9. h. 10. d. 11. l. 12. e. 13. k. 14. g. 15. i.
C. 1. d. 2. b. 3. e. 4. a. 5. d. 6. e. 7. e. 8. d. 9. d. 10. c. 11. a. 12. b. 13. a. 14. e. 15. c.

Lesson XVI

A. 1. preamble. 2. postpone. 3. prediction. 4. posthumous. 5. pretentious. 6. primary. 7. primeval. 8. primogeniture. 9. precept. 10. postscript. 11. precocious. 12. prefabricated. 13. primal. 14. premeditated. 15. postmortem. 16. posterity. 17. primate. 18. preclude. 19. presume. 20. premature.
B. 1. n. 2. r. 3. c. 4. a. 5. e. 6. d. 7. h. 8. q. 9. m. 10. i. 11. k. 12. p. 13. s. 14. b. 15. t. 16. j. 17. g. 18. f. 19. l. 20. o.
C. 1. e. 2. a. 3. e. 4. e. 5. c. 6. c. 7. c. 8. a. 9. e. 10. e. 11. a. 12. b. 13. e. 14. a. 15. e. 16. b. 17. b. 18. e. 19. a. 20. a.

ANSWER KEY

Test 3

1. interjection   d. exclamation
2. internecine   b. internal
3. interregnum   c. period between governments
4. interstices   a. cracks
5. Intervene   e. step in
6. magnate   c. powerful person
7. magnitude   d. extent
8. malevolent   a. malicious
9. malign   c. evil
10. malodorous   d. stinking
11. obdurate   b. hardened
12. obsequious a. servile
13. obtrude   b. impose
14. obviate   c. remove
15. omniscient   e. all knowing
16. percolates   d. brews
17. permeable   b. penetrable
18. pernicious   a. harmful
19. perpetuate   c. prolong
20. pertinent   d. relevant
21. posthumous   b. after death
22. precept   a. principle
23. precocious   c. intelligent
24. primal   d. fundamental
25. primeval   d. ancient

Lesson XVII

A. 1. proceed. 2. prohibit. 3. prospect. 4. prodigal. 5. proponent. 6. procession. 7. provoke. 8. profuse. 9 propulsion. 10. protracted . 11. profit. 12. protruded. 13. pronounce. 14. prominent. 15. profane. 16. procrastinate. 17. propensity. 18. procure. 19. proficient. 20. procedure.
B. 1. k. 2. l. 3. t. 4. o. 5. j. 6. n. 7. c. 8. p. 9. g. 10. r. 11. e. 12. a. 13. q. 14. i. 15. f. 16. h. 17. d. 18. s. 19. b. 20. m.
C. 1. c. 2. d. 3. b. 4. a. 5. a. 6. d. 7. e. 8. c. 9. b. 10. a. 11. c. 12. b. 13. a. 14. d. 15. c. 16. b. 17. a. 18. c. 19. d. 20. c.

Lesson XVIII

A. 1. recite. 2. repatriated. 3. repose. 4. retroactive. 5. reiterated. 6. reimbursed. 7. reticent. 8. retrospect. 9. recognized. 10. recline. 11. retorted. 12. refuted. 13. retrograde. 14. renown. 15. reconciled.
B. 1. k. 2. n. 3. o. 4. i. 5. b. 6. d. 7. f. 8. a. 9. h. 10. l. 11. m. 12. g. 13. e. 14. c. 15. j.
C. 1. e. 2. c. 3. a. 4. b. 5. a. 6. c. 7. b. 8. c. 9. e. 10. b. 11. e. 12. d. 13. c. 14. e. 15. b.

ANSWER KEY

Lesson XIX

A. 1. superseded. 2. secluded. 3. segregation. 4. seduced. 5. secure. 6. supervised. 7. supercilious. 8. superfluous. 9. superlative. 10. sedition.
B. 1. f. 2. d. 3. a. 4. i. 5. e. 6. j. 7. c. 8. h. 9. b. 10. g.
C. 1. a. 2. c. 3. d. 4. b. 5. d. 6. a. 7. b. 8. d. 9. a. 10. d.

Lesson XX

A. 1. substance. 2. succumbed. 3. subjugated. 4. suppress. 5. suggested. 6. subpoena. 7. subjective. 8. submerge. 9. substantiate. 10. suborn. 11. subservient. 12. submarine. 13. suffocate. 14. subterfuge. 15. subordinate. 16. suffused. 17. sublimate. 18. subvert. 19. subscribe. 20. suspended.
B. 1. h. 2. k. 3. c. 4. l. 5. g. 6. q. 7. p. 8. o. 9. r. 10. f. 11. s. 12. n. 13. b. 14. e. 15. i. 16. a. 17. t. 18. m. 19. d. 20. j.
C. 1. c. 2. b. 3. c. 4. a. 5. c. 6. c. 7. d. 8. b. 9. e. 10. c. 11. b. 12. e. 13. d. 14. b. 15. c. 16. b. 17. a. 18. d. 19. c. 20. c.

Lesson XXI

A. 1. trisect. 2. transfixed. 3. viceroy. 4. transmute. 5. unanimous. 6. transcended. 7. uniform. 8. translucent. 9. unify. 10. ultramarine. 11. transcribe. 12. trinity. 13. ultramundane. 14. transitory. 15. unity. 16. transpired. 17. unison. 18. transgress. 19. triumvirate. 20. transparent.
B. 1. k. 2. o. 3. b. 4. q. 5. j. 6. n. 7. i. 8. p. 9. s. 10. h. 11. d. 12. a. 13. t. 14. e. 15. r. 16. l. 17. f. 18. g. 19. m. 20. c.
C. 1. c. 2. b. 3. d. 4. a. 5. b. 6. b. 7. d. 8. b. 9. a. 10. c. 11. b. 12. d. 13. c. 14. d. 15. a. 16. b. 17. c. 18. a. 19. d. 20. e.

Test 4

1. procrastinate — a. postpone
2. prodigal — c. extravagant
3. profane — b. secular
4. propensity — d. tendency
5. protrude — e. bulge
6. reconcile — b. restore peace
7. reiterate — c. repeat
8. reticent — a. silent
9. retort — c. reply rudely
10. retrospect — d. review
11. sedition — b. rebellion
12. segregation — d. separation
13. supercilious — a. haughty
14. superfluous — c. unnecessary
15. supersede — b. replace
16. subjugate — e. control
17. suborn — b. bribe
18. substantiate — d. prove
19. suffuse — c. spread over
20. transcend — a. surpass
21. transmute — c. transform
22. transpire — d. happen
23. triumvirate — c. threesome
24. unanimous — b. in complete agreement
25. unison — e. in one voice

Quiz 1
1. Ambiguous
2. Contraband
3. Abhor
4. Adapt
5. Accord
6. Contrast
7. Adversary
8. Benediction
9. Benefactor
10. Bisect

Quiz 2
1. Duplicate
2. Collide
3. Evokes
4. Eradicate
5. Demented
6. Inscription
7. Equivalent
8. Implicate
9. Distorted
10. Decadent

Quiz 3
1. Perforate
2. Intervene
3. Obliterate
4. Magnificent
5. Illiterate
6. Perspective
7. Multitude
8. Malicious
9. Obsess
10. Interjection

Quiz 4
1. Translucent
2. Primary
3. Recline
4. Provoke
5. Retrospect
6. Subscribe
7. Presume
8. Proceed
9. Postpone
10. Supervise

INDEX

abdicate, 7
abduct, 7
abhor, 7
abject, 7
abjure, 7
abominate, 8
abrasion, 8
abrogate, 8
abrupt, 8
abscess, 8
abscond, 8
absolve, 8
absorb, 8
abstain, 8
abstemious, 8
abstruse, 8
abuse, 9
accord, 15
adaptable, 15
adequate, 15
adhere, 16
ad hoc, 16
adjacent, 16
adjoin, 16
admonish, 16
adopt, 16
advent, 16
adversary, 16
adverse, 16
affliction, 16
aggregation, 17
ambidextrous, 24
ambiguous, 24
ambivalent, 24
annexation, 17
antebellum, 24
antecedent, 25
antedate, 25
antediluvian, 25
ante meridian, 25
anterior, 25

anticipate, 25
appear, 17
appease, 17
arraignment, 17
assimilate, 17
assumption, 17
averse, 9
avert, 9
avocation, 9
benediction, 29
benefactor, 29
beneficent, 29
benevolence, 29
benign, 29
bicameral, 29
biceps, 29
bicuspid, 30
bifurcate, 30
bilateral, 30
bilingual, 30
bipartisan, 30
bisect, 30
bona fide, 30
bonus, 30
circuitous, 35
circulate, 35
circumference, 35
circumlocution, 35
circumnavigate, 35
circumscribe, 36
circumspect, 36
circumstantial, 36
circumvent, 36
coalesce, 41
coherent, 41
collaborate, 41
collateral, 41
collision, 42
collusion, 42
commerce, 42
commiserate, 42

commission, 42
composition, 42
concoct, 42
concord, 42
condone, 42
conference, 42
congenital, 42
consecrate, 43
contraband, 36
contraceptive, 36
contradict, 36
contrast, 36
contravene, 36
contrite, 43
controversy, 36
convene, 43
correspondent, 43
corroborate, 43
debase, 53
decadence, 53
deciduous, 53
dedicate, 53
deflation, 53
demented, 54
demolish, 54
demote, 54
depend, 54
dependent, 54
depreciate, 54
descendant, 54
describe, 54
desiccate, 54
despise, 54
despondent, 54
deter, 55
deviate, 55
devious, 55
devour, 55
diffident, 61
dilapidated, 61
discern, 61

INDEX

discontent, 61
discord, 62
discredit, 62
discrepancy, 62
disintegrate, 62
dispel, 62
dissent, 62
dissident, 62
distortion, 62
distract, 62
diverge, 62
dual, 63
duet, 63
duo, 63
duplex, 63
duplicate, 63
duplicity, 63
elaborate, 69
emigrate, 69
eminent, 69
enervate, 69
equilateral, 70
equilibrium, 70
equity, 71
equivalent, 71
eradicate, 70
erosion, 70
evoke, 70
excise, 70
exclusive, 70
exhilarate, 70
exonerate, 70
exorbitant, 70
extracurricular, 71
extraneous, 71
extravagant, 71
extrovert, 71
illegible, 85
illiterate, 85
illuminate, 77
illustrate, 77
imbibe, 77
immaculate, 85
immature, 85
immigrate, 77
imminent, 79
impeccable, 86
impel, 79
implacable, 86
implicate, 79

impugn, 79
impunity, 86
inaccessible, 86
incarcerate, 79
incessant, 86
incise, 79
inclusive, 79
indorse, 79
induct, 79
inefficient, 86
inflexible, 86
ingratitude, 86
inhospitable, 86
inordinate, 86
inscribe, 79
insoluble, 86
insubordinate, 87
insurgent, 79
intend, 80
intercede, 98
interest, 98
interjection, 98
interlude, 98
intermediary, 99
intermission, 99
intermittent, 99
international, 99
internecine, 99
interpolate, 99
interpret, 99
interregnum, 99
intersect, 99
interstice, 99
intervene, 99
intramural, 100
intravenous, 100
introduce, 100
introspection, 100
introvert, 100
invite, 80
invocation, 80
irradiate, 80
irregular, 87
irrelevant, 87
irreverent, 87
irrevocable, 87
magnanimous, 105
magnate, 105
magnificent, 105
magnitude, 105

majority, 106
maladjusted, 106
malady, 106
malaise, 106
malediction, 106
malefactor, 106
malevolent, 106
malicious, 106
malign, 106
malignant, 106
malnutrition, 106
malodorous, 107
malpractice, 107
multifarious, 107
multilateral, 107
multitude, 107
obdurate, 113
obfuscate, 113
obligation, 113
obliterate, 113
obnoxious, 114
obsequious, 114
obsess, 114
obstacle, 114
obstinate, 114
obtrude, 114
obviate, 114
omnipotent, 114
omnipresent, 114
omniscient, 114
omnivorous, 114
percolate, 119
perfection, 119
perforate, 119
permeable, 119
permission, 120
permutation, 120
pernicious, 120
perpetuate, 120
perplex, 120
persevere, 120
perspective, 120
perspicacious, 120
perspire, 120
pertinent, 121
perturb, 121
posterity, 125
posthumous, 125
postmortem, 125
postpone, 125

INDEX

preamble, 126
precept, 126
preclude, 126
precocious, 126
prediction, 126
prefabricated, 126
premature, 126
premeditated, 126
presume, 126
pretentious, 126
primal, 126
primary, 127
primate, 127
primeval, 127
primogeniture, 127
procedure, 137
proceed, 137
procession, 137
procrastinate, 137
procure, 138
prodigal, 138
profane, 138
proficient, 138
profit, 138
profuse, 138
prohibit, 138
prominent, 138
pronounce, 138
propensity, 138
proponent, 138
propulsion, 139
prospect, 139
protract, 139
protrude, 139

provoke, 139
recite, 145
recline, 145
recognize, 145
reconcile, 145
refute, 146
reimburse, 146
reiterate, 146
renown, 146
repatriate, 146
repose, 146
reticent, 146
retort, 146
retroactive, 146
retrograde, 146
retrospect, 147
seclude, 151
secure, 151
sedition, 151
seduce, 152
segregation, 152
subjective, 157
subjugate, 157
sublimate, 157
submarine, 157
submerge, 158
subordinate, 158
suborn, 158
subpoena, 158
subscribe, 158
subservient, 158
substance, 158
substantiate, 158
subterfuge, 158

subvert, 158
succumb, 159
suffocate, 159
suffuse, 159
suggest, 159
supercilious, 152
superfluous, 152
superlative, 152
supersede, 152
supervise, 152
suppress, 159
suspend, 159
transcend, 165
transcribe, 165
transfix, 165
transgress, 166
transitory, 166
translucent, 166
transmute, 166
transparent, 166
transpire, 166
trinity, 166
trisect, 166
triumvirate, 166
ultramarine, 166
ultramundane, 167
unanimous, 167
uniform, 167
unify, 167
unison, 167
unity, 167
viceroy, 167

www.ingramcontent.com/pod-product-compliance
Lightning Source LLC
Chambersburg PA
CBHW060314240426
43661CB00059B/2764